The Catholic Parish

Shifting Membership in a Changing Church

by
Thomas P. Sweetser, SJ

166498

C
S
S
R

Center for the Scientific Study of Religion

Chicago, Illinois

STUDIES IN RELIGION AND SOCIETY

Center for the Scientific Study of Religion

For a complete list of the publications in the
series, see the back of the book.

Copyright © 1974, Center for the Scientific Study of Religion

Printed in the United States of America

Center for the Scientific Study of Religion
5757 University Avenue
Chicago, Illinois 60637

I S B N: 0-913348-06-6

Library of Congress Catalog Card Number: 74-84543

DEDICATION

To my Mother, without whose prayers and support,

this project would have floundered long ago.

TABLE OF CONTENTS

ACKNOWLEDGEMENTS

A work of this nature, although it carries but one name, is really the work of many. This mention of but a few of the many who have labored through coding, reading, praying, and hoping is a way of saying thank you to all who helped, a way that falls far short of expressing the gratitude I feel.

First mention belongs to Dr. W. Widick Schroeder who introduced me to this project by asking me to join in a study of religious attitudes and practices in the southwest suburbs of Chicago. Not only did he introduce me to this project but he advised me in its design and progress and corrected the results as they unfolded in this volume. As my advisor and director of research, I am indebted to him for his patience and concern.

Mention is also due Dr. Victor Obenhaus and Dr. Thomas C. Campbell, who have helped me form my ideas and have suggested corrections and additions as my work progressed.

And finally, there is the long list of people who have read and corrected my work. Special mention is due Ruth Kleitsch OSF, Ann Leadon, Marion Garvey, James Ewens SJ, Jane Gerard CSJ, Mary New, Kathleen Hage, Kathleen McDonald CSJ, and Marguerite Corcoran CSJ, who designed the cover for the paper-back edition, plus so many more. My thanks to you all!

vi

LIST OF TABLES

CHAPTER I

CHAPTER II

CHAPTER III

CHAPTER IV

CHAPTER V

APPENDICES

LIST OF FIGURES

CHAPTER I

THE PARISH:

CHOOSING A SAMPLE

This book deals with shifting membership patterns in the
American Catholic parish since Vatican II: their extent and direction
and the reasons why they are occurring at this time in the Church.
Studies of the American Catholic Church and parish affiliation conducted
in recent years have agreed on one fact: the percentage of people who
are active in the parish is smaller now than it was ten or even five
years ago.[1]

But although studies agree on the fact of withdrawal, there is
little information on the extent of the withdrawal from parish participation or what types of people are likely to be less active now than
they once were. The purpose of this volume is to provide information
based on a group of Catholic parishes which can be used as a comparison
for other parish situations throughout the country.

The study was not a large one, certainly not of the scope of the
national study of American Catholic clergy commissioned by the bishops
and conducted by Fr. Andrew Greeley (1972). But although it was not a
national survey, a great deal of care and planning were involved in
finding a study area and a group of parishes that could provide a representative cross-section of Catholic practice and opinion.[2]

The study area that was selected consisted of eight suburban
communities in the Chicago metropolitan area (See Figure 1-1). Of the
eight communities chosen, half were older urban areas, characterized by
heavy industry, ethnic populations, and sections analogous to inner areas
of a large city. The other half were more recent developments and included
middle or upper middle class life-styles.

Satellite City, for instance, is a manufacturing center containing
steel foundries and forging mills. Shopton, adjacent to Satellite City

1

Figure 1-1:   THE EIGHT COMMUNITIES OF
              THE STUDY AREA

Note:

1.   The names used are
     fictitious.

2.   The populations given
     are those of the 1970
     census.

3.   The communities
     are numbered in
     order of socio-
     economic rank,
     beginning with
     the lowest.

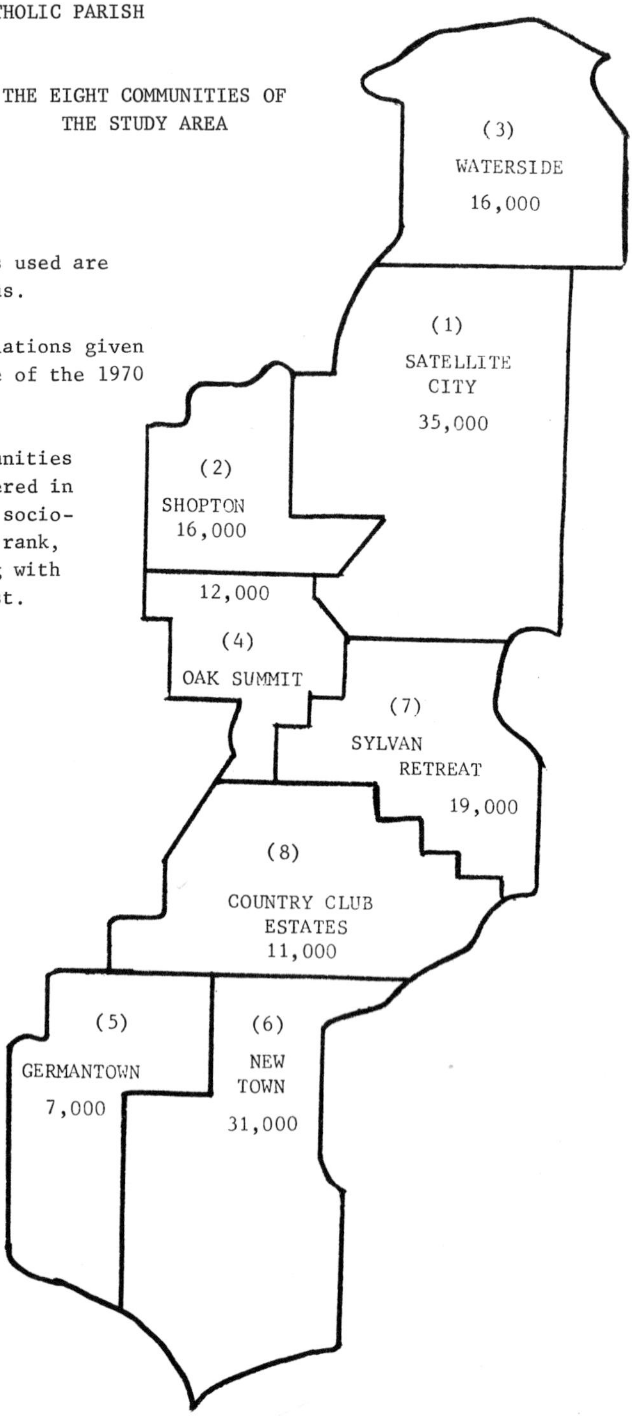

(3)
WATERSIDE
16,000

(1)
SATELLITE
CITY
35,000

(2)
SHOPTON
16,000

12,000

(4)
OAK SUMMIT

(7)
SYLVAN
RETREAT
19,000

(8)
COUNTRY CLUB
ESTATES
11,000

(5)
GERMANTOWN
7,000

(6)
NEW
TOWN
31,000

is over 50 percent black. Both of these communities rank in the lower third of the socioeconomic scale when compared with other communities in the Chicago area.

Waterside and Oak Summit, the communities on either side of the first two, rank in income and educational background near the medium for the metropolitan area. Waterside is an older, stable residential area containing few blacks and having the largest percentage of people over the age of sixty-five (11 percent) in the study area.

Oak Summit, on the other hand, has a much younger and more fluid population. It acts as a buffer zone between the predominantly blue collar community of Shopton and the more affluent Sylvan Retreat. Oak Summit's population increased 58 percent between 1960 and 1970, whereas Waterside increased only 32 percent.

A community much like Oak Summit is the new community on the far edge of the study area, Germantown. It has the same medium family income and educational level as Oak Summit, but is only beginning to develop. The 1970 population of 7,000 was a 76 percent increase over 1960, and there are still large areas of land available for development.

New Town, on the other hand, has little land left for development. It was a carefully planned community which has now reached the limit of expansion. And yet, despite its physical stability, there is still a rapid change-over of families that are moving in and out. The reason for this is that it is made up mostly of young, professional, and lower management people. For this reason the medium family income is comparable to Oak Summit and Germantown, but the average educational level is much higher. It is, in other words, a "port-of-entry" for well-educated, young married adults who are not likely to settle down in New Town. Once their position and salary permit, they most likely will move to a more prestigeous community such as Sylvan Retreat or Country Club Estates.

These last two communities, Sylvan Retreat and Country Club Estates, rank in the upper third of the socioeconomic and educational levels of the Chicago metropolitan communities. The medium family income for Country Club Estates in 1970 was $26,400 and the average number of years of schooling completed by people twenty-five or over was fifteen years. Country Club Estates, in other words, is made up of a group of highly successful professional people and business executives. Sylvan Retreat, while not as affluent or as well-educated as Country Club Estates, is still above average in the income spectrum and in the percentage of professionals living in the community. It contains an older and more settled populace than Country Club Estates.

TABLE 1-1

STATISTICAL DATA ON THE STUDY AREA

	Income	Education	Age	Percent Black	Percent Professional	Percent Catholic
	Medium Income (1970)	Years of School Completed for People 25 and Over	Medium (1970)	(1970)	Percent of Labor Force Professionally Employed	Percent of Population Catholic
Satellite City	11,000	11.7	26.2	31	10.1	28 (24% White, 4% Black)
Shopton	12,000	12.0	20.2	50	10.1	50 (40% White, 10% Black)
Waterside	12,500	12.3	31.1	0	18.4	61
Oak Summit	14,100	12.5	25.3	0	19.6	61
Germantown	14,000	12.5	24.8	2	21.1	35
New Town	14,000	13.1	25.6	2	31.4	32
Sylvan Retreat	15,800	12.8	33.9	0	24.8	39
Country Club Estates	26,400	14.8	31.5	0	33.6	30
Chicago Metropolitan						

Table 1-1 gives a comparison of the communities used in the study. We have tried to show by this table and in this description of the area that these communities contain a wide variety of social, economic, educational, and ethnic backgrounds and in this sense represent the same variety found in any larger metropolitan area.

The Catholic Population

The original study included all the Catholic, Protestant and Jewish clergy serving churches or synagogues in the area, as well as a sampling of Catholic, Protestant and Jewish lay opinion. This report will concentrate on the Catholic response.

There were ten Catholic parishes included within the eight communities studied. Three of the ten were in Satellite City and at one time served a Catholic ethnic population that migrated to the area to work in the factories of the city. These parishes have been affected in recent years by the shift from a white to a black population in Satellite City. Because of this shift the membership in recent years has dropped in the parishes. The parochial schools attached to the parishes reflect the change in the growing number of non-Catholic black students attending the schools.

The same is true for the parish in Shopton which serves blue collar parishioners living in the area. Although the community is still predominantly Catholic, the religious makeup of the town is changing as it becomes a predominantly black community. This in turn has had a profound effect on the parish membership.

The parish in Waterside, on the other hand, is much more stable. It serves an older population who have moved there from other communities which are now predominantly black. For the time being the parish is well-supported and growing, but this will probably change in a decade or two as the older population dies out and other black and ethnic groups move into the area.

The parish in Oak Summit serves a lower, middle class white population. It is in between a predominantly black community on one side and a more affluent, professional community on the other. The parish reflects this mobile and somewhat unsettled character of the community. The church itself is in the gymnasium of the school, and the priests live in two neighborhood houses near the parish.

The Germantown parish, while serving the same type of community as Oak Summit, has a much smaller number of Catholics to contend with. The difference, however, is that Germantown is a new community and is growing rapidly. As a result, the parish has constructed a large church and school in anticipation of a large Catholic migration.

The situation is quite different for the parish in New Town. The community, although highly mobile, has reached the limit of its physical development. As a result, the parish can predict the size of the Catholic population with some accuracy. Its biggest problem is dealing with the continual change-over of membership. There is no parochial school attached to the parish, and religious education of the children is handled through a catechetical center run by the parish and staffed by lay volunteers. Since there is such a high educational level in the community, finding qualified teachers is not so difficult as providing continuity in the program where there is a rapid change-over of personnel.

The parishes in each of the two upper-status communities, Sylvan Retreat and Country Club Estates, are well-established and thriving. They have large parish plants, well-staffed schools and a wide variety of parish programs. The Country Club Estates parish has an active program of lay involvement and a variety of liturgical forms available for parishioners of varying tastes. The Sylvan Retreat parish serves an older and not as professionally-oriented Catholic community but it still gives the impression of being a self-sustaining and successful operation.

This description of the parishes included within the study area is presented here to indicate the variety of Catholics included in the study. It was hoped that this sample would include the various types and sub-groups of Catholics found in any metropolitan area and would contain the same variety of Catholic attitudes and practices.

The one noticeable exception is the lack of representation from the Catholics of Latin background, a group that now makes up 25 percent of the nation's Catholic population. The character of this group and their position in the American culture is so unique that it was felt that they deserved separate and special attention. It is hoped that studies will be conducted to deal with the needs and expectations of the Latin Catholic population of our country. Unfortunately, our study was not able to deal with this significant Catholic minority.

Sampling Procedures

The sampling procedures involved two stages: the sampling of
the clergy and a random sampling of the laity. The first stage consisted
of a questionnaire mailed to all the Catholic, Protestant and Jewish
clergy within the study area. Included in this sampling were twenty-four
resident Catholic priests and one sister employed as a full-time parish
staff member. The clergy were asked to fill out the questionnaire and
give the completed form to an interviewer who would call on them approximately two weeks after they received the questionnaire. The sister
and twenty-one of the priests agreed to fill out the questionnaire and
to be interviewed.

Two pastors and one associate pastor refused to cooperate with
the survey. The reason given was they were too busy and could not be
bothered. There was no indication, however, that these three refusals
came from an attitude or position not represented in the data received
from the other priests. From the responses of the twenty-one priests
and one sister who did respond to the survey the data reported in Chapters
II through IV involving the Catholic clergy were drawn. A valuable
secondary source was also available for comparison, namely, the national
survey of American Catholic priests conducted for the National Conference
of Catholic Bishops by Andrew Greeley. That project was undertaken at
the same time as our own study.

The second stage involved a survey of a random sample of Catholic
laity. The resources of the project did not permit a sampling of all
the parishes in the area. Instead, three representative parishes were
selected for the lay sample.

The three parishes were from three different socioeconomic status
communities. One parish was in Satellite City. It served a decreasing
population of white ethnic and blue collar Catholics, mostly of Eastern
European origin, as well as a small percentage of blacks residing in the
area.

The second parish served the young, professional community of
New Town. This provided a sampling of middle income, younger Catholic
parishioners. The third parish was in the affluent Country Club Estates
community serving an upper status and older Catholic population. By
taking a random sample of the parishioners from these three parishes, a
cross-section of lower, middle and higher socioeconomic status Catholics
was obtained without involving a large number of people in the sample
itself.

TABLE 1-2

SAMPLE SIZE AND RESPONSE RATES OF THE CATHOLIC LAITY

Questionnaires Mailed	Satellite City		New Town		Country Club Estates		Total Response	
	No.	Pct.	No.	Pct.	No.	Pct.	No.	Pct.
Mailed out	310	100	311	100	323	100	944	100
Dropped (moved, died, incompetent, etc.)	8	3	13	4	10	3	31	3
New totals	302	100	298	100	313	100	913	100
Questionnaire respondents	149	50	201	67	205	65	555	61
Telephone respondents	19	6	25	9	30	10	74	8
Explicit refusals	67	22	25	9	36	12	128	14
Other non-respondents	67	22	47	15	42	13	156	17

Note: Overall Response Rate = 69 percent (questionnaire and phone).

After receiving permission from the pastors of these three parishes, a sample of about 300 names was selected from each of the parishes' membership lists. The sample was drawn using a set of random numbers and the name of any person over the age of seventeen was considered a valid entry.[3]

Table 1-2 gives a breakdown of the sample size and the response rates from each of the parishes. Besides this sample drawn from the three Catholic parishes, the laity from a Methodist parish in each of the three communities were also surveyed, as were two predominantly black churches in Satellite City and two Jewish synagogues in Country Club Estates. The responses from these congregations were used in the larger study and served as a comparison for the Catholic attitudes and practices presented in this volume.

From late January through early March of 1972 numbered questionnaires were mailed out along with a return envelope. A cover letter
urged candor, noted that the pastor's approval had been obtained, and
promised that no individual's response would be seen by the staff or
members of the local church.

The clergy had been assured that no one would be under pressure
to respond, either in the initial contact or in the followup procedures.
Telephone calls were made to non-respondents at two week intervals until
the cut-off date in May or until the person indicated a refusal to participate. Those with unlisted phone numbers were sent postcards as reminders,
and in Satellite City those without telephones were visited personally
to make sure they had received the questionnaire.

This procedure produced a response rate of 75 percent in the
Country Club Estates parish, 76 percent in New Town and 56 percent in
Satellite City. The overall rate was 69 percent. The proportion of
persons who explicitly refused to participate was only 14 percent of the
total sample. The category "Other non-respondents" includes those persons
who did not refuse to participate but who never could "find the time" to
fill out the survey, or who said they had sent it in but it was not
received, or those who could not be reached for a telephone or personal
interview.

This, then, is the description of the Catholic sample that is
reported in succeeding chapters of this book. It has been placed at the
beginning so that the results of the study can be understood and evalu-
ated and can more easily be used as a comparison with parish situations
in other parts of the country. We begin the report with the clergy response from the ten parishes in the study area.

CHAPTER II

THE NORM:

THE RESPONSE OF THE PARISH CLERGY

In seeking to uncover the changes in parish membership over the last few years, the first area of inquiry involves the parish clergy. An excellent study of the American Catholic clergy has been conducted by Andrew Greeley (1972b) and frequent reference to that study will be made throughout this chapter.

But what makes our study unique is the effort to compare the attitudes and opinions of the parish priests with the attitudes and opinions of their people and with the responses of clergymen of other faiths in the same area. In our study of shifting patterns of parish membership the positions of the parish clergy are used as the norm or standard by which to judge the changes in the attitudes and practices of their parishioners. To do this we must first learn something about the opinions of clergy who serve in the parishes of our study area.

An attempt was made in the survey not only to uncover the clergy's own opinions and attitudes on religious, social, and moral issues, but also to learn how they felt the majority of their parishioners would respond to these same issues. The results of the survey will be considered under these four headings: (1) the clergy's identification with the institutional church; (2) their attitudes toward parish ministry; (3) their emphases in the ministry, as well as their own personal and social value orientations; and (4) their estimates of the attitudes of their parishioners.

Church Identity

One indication of the clergy's identification with the institutional Church is their reaction to the changes that have taken place in

_-_ .nce the Second Vatican Council. Table 2-1 gives the Catholic clergy reaction to these changes.

TABLE 2-1

RESPONSES BY PERCENT TO THE QUESTION: WHAT IS YOUR ATTITUDE
TOWARD CHANGES IN THE AMERICAN CATHOLIC CHURCH?

Responses	Catholic Clergy
1. I was satisfied with the pre-Vatican II Church.	0
2. I would like a slower rate of change.	18
3. I am satisfied with the Church's present rate of change.	36
4. I look forward to a more rapid rate of change in the future.	18
5. I feel radical change is necessary in the Church.	23
6. I am confused and uncertain about changes in the church.	5
Total	100

It is evident from these responses that the majority of the
Catholic clergy are in favor of the changes that are going on in the
Church and that 41 percent of them feel that even a faster rate of change
is necessary. Over half of this 41 percent look for radical changes in
the Church. This is in comparison with 31 percent of the Protestant and
Jewish clergy who feel the need for a more rapid rate of change in their
denominations.[1] This seems to indicate that the Catholic clergy are not
opposed to changes and are, as will become evident in the next chapter,
far ahead of their own parishioners in their openness to change. Only
18 percent of the laity were in favor of a more rapid rate of change in
the Church.

To learn the clergy's reaction to the Church more directly, they
were asked how favorable they were toward Catholic beliefs and practices.

Fifty-five percent were very favorable and another 32 percent were favorable, which gives a total positive response of 87 percent. Only one person indicated a negative reaction and another had mixed feelings. Their reaction to the Church's leadership, however, was not as favorable. In responding to the question: "In general, what is your attitude toward position statements on public policy issued by the Archbishop and the Chancery Office?", only 37 percent gave a favorable response, while 36 percent indicated mixed feelings. Of the rest, 9 percent were unfavorable and 18 percent had no opinion one way or another.

When asked whether their attitude toward such policy statements had changed over the past few years, no one indicated that his attitude had become more favorable recently. On the other hand, 18 percent said they were less favorable now than previously. The rest said that their attitude had remained unchanged (68 percent) or that they had no opinion on the matter (14 percent).

This response would seem to indicate that while the clergy are loyal to the beliefs and practices of the Church, they have reservations about statements coming from diocesan officials. But in order better to judge the clergy's attitude toward the Church, more subtle indicators must be considered. One of these is their reaction to parish life and ministry.

Parish Ministry

The great majority of the Catholic clergy like their work in the parish. When asked, "In general, what is your attitude toward your present parish work?" 64 percent were on the favorable side of the response options. When asked whether their attitudes toward parish work had changed over the last few years, again 82 percent of them said their attitudes had not changed or were even more favorable now. This is a vote of confidence for parish work by those who are best able to make such a judgment.

The priests, however, were not as universal in their praise of parish work as were their Protestant and Jewish confreres. Tables 2-2 and 2-3 show the contrast between the two groups.

Notice that none of the Protestant and Jewish groups registered unfavorable opinions toward parish work while 18 percent of the Catholic clergy did. This 18 percent unfavorable response lends support to the national priesthood study that reported ". . . among diocesan priests,

TABLE 2-2

CLERGY ATTITUDES TOWARD PARISH WORK, BY PERCENT

Response	Catholic Clergy (N=22)	Protestant and Jewish Clergy (N=79)
1. Very favorable	18	47
2. Favorable	46	34
3. Mixed feelings	18	15
4. Unfavorable	9	0
5. Very unfavorable	9	0
6. No opinion	0	5
Total	100	101

TABLE 2-3

CHANGES IN CLERGY ATTITUDES TOWARD PARISH WORK
IN THE PAST FEW YEARS, BY PERCENT

Response	Catholic Clergy	Protestant and Jewish Clergy
1. More favorable now	41	36
2. No change	41	43
3. Less favorable now	18	15
4. No opinion	0	6
Total	100	100

the lowest level of job satisfaction is found among associate pastors,
who are lower even than corresponding groups in the American population"
(Greeley, 1972b:191). It is important to consider more closely this job
satisfaction among the parish clergy. In order to do this, we will look
at how they react to various parish activities and functions.

The scope of parish ministry has been greatly altered by the
Second Vatican Council and the changes that have been introduced into
the Church since the Council.[2] Parish councils, school boards, liturgy
committees, scripture study groups, encounter sessions and workshops;
all these have been introduced into parish life within the last ten years.
How do the parish clergy feel about these parish activities and how do
their attitudes compare with their Protestant and Jewish fellow workers?
Table 2-4 summarizes the responses of those who reacted favorably toward
various parish activities. The list includes both traditional and innovative types of activities. They are arranged in order of greatest to
least favorable response by the Catholic clergy.

The Catholic clergy agree with the Protestant and Jewish groups
in their favorable attitude toward religious educational activities and
liturgical groups in the parish. They also agree that the least favored
activities are personal growth groups and fund-raising activities.

It is presumed that the unfavorable reaction to fund-raising
activities (bingo, bake sales, etc.) is due to their time-consuming,
"unreligious" nature. These duties, however, must be endured if the
parish is to remain solvent. As we shall see in the next chapter, the
laity are much more favorably disposed to fund-raising groups. Seventy-
two percent of the parishioners indicated a favorable response. Perhaps
the difference between the clergy and the lay response is the responsibility the clergy feel in financing the parish operation. The laity
are not so burdened and can enjoy the fund-raising events rather than
worrying about their outcome.

The personal growth groups, on the other hand, appear to be re-
garded unfavorably or with mixed feelings by the majority of all ministerial groups. This is perhaps because such activities are a new phenomenon in the parish, and there is a great deal of apprehension and
ambiguous feeling among the clergy as to their place in parish life.
Curiously, however, not all those interested in these movements were
young clergy. Those who said they were favorably disposed to encounter
groups included all ages and had two Catholic pastors among their number.

There is little agreement among the Catholic and the Protestant-
Jewish clergy groups as to the ranking of the other parish activities

TABLE 2-4

CLERGY'S FAVORABLE RESPONSE TOWARD PARISH ACTIVITIES, BY PERCENT

Parish Activity	Catholic Clergy	Protestant and Jewish Clergy	Percentage Difference
1. Adult religious activities	96	94	2
2. Liturgical groups	91	82	9
3. Administrative groups	82	72	10
4. Recreational and social groups	59	41	18
5. Parish service groups	55	76	-21[a]
6. Social action groups	55	56	1
7. Prayer and devotional groups	50	79	-29
8. Parish school	36	No Schools	--
9. Experimental personal growth groups	27	27	0
10. Fund-raising groups	23	18	5

[a]The minus sign indicates that the Protestant-Jewish clergy response was higher than the Catholic clergy response.

found in Table 2-4. Some of the discrepancies are more easily explained than others. For instance, we can understand why the Protestant clergy would be more favorably disposed to prayer meetings and parish devotional groups, since these activities have been closer to the Protestant tradition and a third of the Protestant clergy sampling were from fundamentalist, Bible-oriented churches.[3] There is also the added factor that Catholic novenas and evening devotions have been receding from the parish scene since the liturgical changes that followed Vatican II.

The difference in emphasis between Protestant and Catholic parishes is also apparent in the different reaction to parish service groups. The Protestant clergy have their calendars filled with such activities while the Catholic emphasis has been on Mass schedules and administering the Sacraments.

Why the Catholic clergy should be more favorable toward parish administration groups and recreational groups than other clergy groups is not immediately obvious. The favorable attitudes toward recreational groups among the Catholics may be a carry-over from the days when the Catholic parish was the social center for the surrounding ethnic Catholic population. Such traditions remain long after the ethnic identity of the parish has been absorbed into the larger culture.[4]

The discrepancy in attitudes toward administration groups (parish councils, lay boards, etc.) perhaps can be explained by the fact that the Catholic clergy still have control of the decision-making process while many of the other clergy groups must bow to the power of the parish lay leaders. This becomes apparent in the responses of the clergy when asked about the extent of lay participation in the policy planning of the parish. Not one Catholic pastor indicated that the laity of his parish had full powers for initiating policy in all areas of parish life. Sixty percent of the Protestant pastors said that their laity did have this power.

There are two other interesting aspects of Table 2-4 on clergy attitudes toward parish activities. One is the almost identical reaction of all clergy groups to social action parish groups. Barely half of the clergy reacted favorably to these kinds of activities.[5] Since the survey was conducted in January of 1972, while American troops were still involved in the Vietnam war, and all the clergy interviewed were serving suburban parishes in which racial integration was a touchy issue, opinions appear to be divided as to how the parish was to deal with these social issues. We will see more of these attitudes toward parish involvement in social and political issues in the latter parts of this chapter.

The second interesting aspect of Catholic clergy attitudes is the unfavorable position of the parish school, coming eighth in a list of ten in Table 2-4.[6] The disenchantment with the parish school in this sample was noticeable in the response to the question, "Has your attitude toward the parish school changed over the past few years?" Over 40 percent of the priests responded that their opinions were less favorable to the school at the time of the survey than previously, compared with only 9 percent who said they were more favorable now than previously. One of the parishes, in fact, had closed its school two years before the survey was taken and has since concentrated on a family catechetical approach to religious education.

Strong feelings concerning the parish school were expressed by the Catholic clergy in the interview sessions. Typical comments were: "The school is pulling the parish under." "Separate the school from the parish so people are parish-centered, not school-dominated." "The Catholic school system is social injustice. We take care of the privileged few and use up all the parish funds for the minority."[7]

One final indicator of the Catholic clergy's attitudes toward parish life is their reaction to religious and liturgical activities in the parish. The priests were given a list of liturgical functions ranging from more traditional forms of liturgical activity, such as nonparticipation Masses, to more innovative forms, such as laymen receiving communion in the hand. Table 2-5 indicates those among the Catholic clergy who reacted either favorably or very favorably toward various liturgical functions. The table is arranged in order of greatest to least clergy preference.

It is interesting to note how favorable priests are to the liturgical innovations that have been introduced since the Second Vatican Council. Guitar Masses, Masses in homes and Communal Penance Services were favored by over two-thirds of the clergy. Half of the clergy were in favor of laymen receiving communion in the hand, over a third strongly in favor of this practice. The more traditional practices of Benediction and quiet, non-participation types of liturgy were favored by only two-fifths of the clergy. We will see in the next chapter how striking is the contrast between this response of the clergy and the response of their parishioners.

The Catholic clergy spend by far the majority of their time in parish duties. Only 9 percent of them, as compared with 18 percent of the Protestant and Jewish clergy, spend more than 20 percent of their time in extra-parochial activities and less than a half of the Catholic clergy (45 percent) belong to more than one voluntary organization outside of the parish. Two-thirds of the other clergy groups belong to more than one such organization.

If interest and attachment are measured by the amount of time a person is willing to spend in that activity, then the Catholic clergy score high in their identification with parish life and Church-related activities.

Another way of gauging the clergys' attachments to parish life is to look at their plans for the future. Of the twenty-two Catholic clergy interviewed, fifteen (68 percent) planned to be doing parish work five years from the time of the interview. The remaining seven were

TABLE 2-5

FAVORABLE ATTITUDES OF THE CATHOLIC CLERGY TOWARD
PARISH LITURGICAL FUNCTIONS, BY PERCENT

Liturgical Function	Very Favorable	Favorable	Total Favorable Response
1. Participation Mass with singing	73	23	96
2. Guitar Mass with contemporary hymns	46	36	82
3. Informal Masses in homes	50	23	73
4. Prayer groups and services	32	41	73
5. Communal penance services	41	27	68
6. Laymen distributing communion	27	41	68
7. The "Kiss-of-Peace" in Mass	32	32	64
8. Baptisms during Mass	27	32	59
9. Laymen receiving communion in the hand	36	14	50
10. Mass with no singing but with responses	4	36	40
11. Benediction and evening devotions	4	36	40
12. Quiet Mass with no singing or responses	0	9	9

divided among religious teaching, hospital work, chaplaincy in the Armed Forces and retirement.

As a check to see what in fact had happened to the respondents, a telephone call was made six months following the interviews to see what changes had occurred in that short time. The results showed that of the twenty-two contacted, fifteen (68 percent) were still at their original posts. Of the remaining seven, one had retired as planned, two had al-

ready gone into full-time religious teaching, one had joined the Armed
Forces Chaplaincy as he had planned, one was on sick leave, one had re-
quested and received a transfer to another parish outside of the study
area and one had left the priesthood. As a result, of the original
twenty-two respondents, sixteen still remained in parish work, a drop
of 27 percent in six months!

It is impossible to judge from so small a sample whether this
drop in Catholic clergy serving in parish ministry is part of a larger
trend.[8] From the internal evidence of their own attitudes toward parish
work, and toward the Church in general, they appear to be dedicated and
loyal servants of the Church. They also said they experienced support
from their parishioners. Eighty-six percent of the Catholic clergy reported that they felt the majority of their people were favorable toward
themselves and their work.

There are other indications, however, that make one wonder
whether the parish clergy are that satisfied with what they are doing.
Andrew Greeley reports in his analysis of the national priesthood study
that ". . . the condition of the associate pastor is poor. Job satisfaction in this group, for example, is generally lower than that of un-
skilled workers" (Greeley, 1972b:313).[9]

Our survey also uncovered dissatisfactions among the Catholic
clergy. The fact that so many expressed disfavor with diocesan pro-
nouncements and a significant number were looking into other types of
ministries is an indication of this discontent. While there are many
reasons for discontent, some of it may stem from the gap the clergy
feel between their own attitudes toward parish life and the attitudes
of their people. To learn whether this is the case we will now look at
some of the value orientations and emphases in the ministry among the
Catholic clergy.

Emphases in the Ministry and Value Orientations

We begin with a look at what things the Catholic clergy feel are
important to emphasize in their sermons, teaching, and counseling. Table
2-6 indicates which subjects are most often emphasized.

The order of emphasis agrees with the Protestant-Jewish response
with one notable exception. The Catholic clergy give more time in their
teaching and preaching to giving direction concerning social and political issues, 63 percent for the Catholics versus 54 percent for the other
groups.[10] Catholic clergy give less time, however, to preaching on

business ethics, 60 percent versus 78 percent. And while giving direction in prayer and holiness comes third in both lists, the Protestant-
Jewish responses showed a greater stress on these subjects.

TABLE 2-6

CLERGY'S EMPHASIS ON VARIOUS TOPICS OF INSTRUCTION, BY PERCENT,
RANKED BY TOTAL EMPHASIS OF THE CATHOLIC CLERGY

Topic	Much Emphasis	Some Emphasis	Total Emphasis	Total Protestant and Jewish Emphasis
1. Giving direction in theology and scrip-ture	59	36	95	87
2. Giving direction in family and marital problems	23	55	78	87
3. Giving direction in personal prayer and holiness	18	50	68	80
4. Giving direction in social and politi-cal issues	18	45	63	54
5. Giving direction in business ethics	5	55	60	78

Table 2-6 indicates which topics are most often mentioned in
sermons and instruction classes, but it does not give an idea of the
direction this emphasis takes. It is to this question that we now turn.

First, in the area of theology and scripture, there are indications from the Catholic clergy responses that the majority follow middle-
of-the-road interpretations of post-Vatican II thought. The interviews

revealed, for instance, that the respondents were not avid readers of new theology, but neither did they hang on to antiquated theological opinions.[11]

They were in favor of changes that have taken place in the Church since Vatican II but have little time to keep up with current theological discussion. Their understanding of scripture follows the orthodox Catholic teaching that scripture is not literally true but is one of many ways of knowing about God. Thirty-seven percent replied that "Scripture is not literally true but is the most important way of knowing about God," while 45 percent responded that "Scripture is one of many equally important ways of knowing about God." The rest wrote in their own responses which were similar to these two responses.

This emphasis of the Catholic clergy on scripture as one of many ways to God--others being tradition, the Sacraments, the Mass, etc.-- provides some indication of what direction the priests' emphasis on theology and scripture takes in their preaching and instruction.

The second greatest emphasis is on family and marital problems. There were indications from other questions asked in the survey what direction this emphasis would take. One such indicator was the response to the question, "In general, which of the following ways of making fami- ly decisions do you think is most desirable?" Half of the Catholic clergy indicated that the husband and wife together should make the major decisions. Only 34 percent of the other clergy groups felt this way. Nearly a third of the Catholic group (32 percent) felt that parents should consult their children about major decisions. Twenty-four percent of the other clergy thought this was best. About equal proportions of all clergy groups (18 percent of the Catholics versus 21 percent of the other groups) felt that the family as a group should make the decisions. The difference between the Catholic and non-Catholic clergy came in the response to the option that the husband should make all the major decisions himself. None of the priests responded in this way, while 11 percent of the Prot- estant and Jewish groups picked this response. We will see in the next chapter how this compared with the Catholic lay response to this question. But we do have some idea of the attitude the Catholic clergy assume in their direction of the laity. It appears to take a democratic, egali- tarian bent which is confirmed by other of their responses.

For instance, in their attitudes toward raising children, half of them felt that the most important thing for a child to learn in order to prepare himself for life was to think for himself. Another 27 per- cent felt the most important thing to learn was to help others when they are in need. Only 18 percent felt the most important thing to teach the child was to obey. The clergy's emphasis, then, seems to be in developing independence rather than in obeying authority. This agrees with the Protestant-Jewish clergy response, with the one exception that learning to be of service to others in need received much less emphasis among Protestant-Jewish groups. Only 18 percent of them so responded, compared with a 27 percent response from the Catholic clergy.

The third most emphasized subject was giving direction in personal prayer and holiness. Here again we can learn a little about how the priests treated this subject, although this area of personal spirituality is much more subtle and difficult to get at. As the report to the American bishops on Priestly Spiritual Renewal mentions: "My sermons, for example, are vibrant with the pulsation of life because I preach, not a doctrine, but the Christ who is really the Lord of my life" (Larkin, O. Carm. and Broccolo, 1973:58). When a person preaches on prayer and holiness, in other words, it comes from one's own experience of this reality. One glimpse into this area is how the clergy themselves experience God's presence. Table 2-7 gives the clergy's response to the question, "As an adult, have you ever had a personal experience of the Presence of God?"

TABLE 2-7

THE CLERGY'S EXPERIENCE OF THE PRESENCE OF GOD, BY PERCENT

Response	Catholic Clergy	Protestant and Jewish Clergy
1. I am sure I have	36	82
2. I think I have	36	11
3. I don't think so	14	3
4. I am sure I have not	0	1
5. No response	13	3
Total	100	100

This discrepancy between the Catholic and other clergy groups' response, as well as the greater emphasis that the Protestant clergy place on personal prayer in their sermons and ministry, indicates a uniqueness in the Catholic tradition toward the experience of the Presence of God. Because of the importance of the Mass in Catholic worship and the objective character of the Real Presence in the Eucharist, the subjective elements of the Personal Presence of God have not been given the same emphasis as they have in the other traditions. This may be changing, however, with the appearance of the Catholic Pentecostal Movement. What effect this will have on parish ministry has yet to be determined.[12]

It is also possible to give some indication of the Catholic clergy's emphasis on social and political issues. As Table 2-6 indicated, two-thirds of the Catholic clergy emphasized these issues in their ministry. The next question, of course is what did they say about these issues.

One indication of their emphasis is the role they see the local parish taking in social and political concerns. Should the parish take an official stand on such issues? Should it form parish discussion groups on public policy or only encourage parishioners to join local community activities?

All the Catholic respondents agreed that at the very least, parishioners should be encouraged to participate in community action groups. Almost all of them (82 percent) also agreed that discussion groups should be formed in the parish on public policy issues. A large majority (73 percent) agreed that the parish facilities should be allowed to be used for community action groups. The line was drawn, however, at the parish taking an official stand on public policy issues. Only 36 percent agreed to this measure and even fewer (23 percent) agreed to the formation of parish-sponsored social action groups.

These views were substantiated in the interview material. The respondents were given the opportunity to give an open-ended reply to the question, "What contribution do you think the Catholic Church should make to American culture?" The predominant opinion was that the Church provides the principles which individuals are able to use in particular situations. The emphasis was on providing a good example rather than on direct intervention and action. Only the younger clergy said the Church should become actively involved in social and political issues. Three of the four who so responded were under thirty years old. The older clergy, on the other hand, said that the Church should keep its hands out of politics and should emphasize instead the spiritual development of its people. There was one exception to this position of neutrality toward politics among the Catholic clergy that was in direct contrast to the other clergy. It involved government aid to Church-sponsored schools. Seventy-three percent of the Catholic compared with only 7 percent of the other clergy were in favor of this action. That's a difference of 67 percent!

And yet, the vast majority of all clergy groups, Catholic, Protestant, and Jewish, agreed that the government should remain neutral toward religious institutions. Seventy-seven percent of the Catholics and 78 percent of the other clergy groups agreed with this position. It would appear, then, that the Catholic clergy, in seeking public aid for private education, consider this as providing an educational alternative to the public school system and not a state subsidy of the Catholic religion.

This is such an important issue, i.e., the position of the Church's ministers on social questions, that it is worthwhile looking at the clergy's own value orientations. A few representative social issues were selected as an indication of where they stand. Table 2-8 gives the responses of the clergy to various social issues.

TABLE 2-8

CLERGY AGREEMENT TO SOCIAL AND POLITICAL STATEMENTS, BY PERCENT,
RANKED IN ORDER OF TOTAL AGREEMENT BY THE CATHOLIC CLERGY

| Statement | Catholic Clergy | | | Other Clergy |
	Strongly Agree	Agree	Total Agreement	Total Agreement
1. Christian principles can provide a basis for protest movements	23	59	82	53
2. Parishes should try to include all races and peoples	27	50	77	61
3. Suburbs should be racially integrated	36	41	77	67
4. American involvement in Vietnam has been immoral	14	23	37	43

It appears from this table that a large majority of the Catholic clergy support integration both of their neighborhood and of the parishes. Their Protestant and Jewish confreres are not so universally in favor of this measure. Although 86 percent of the black clergy thought the suburbs should be integrated, only 48 percent of the fundamentalist clergy did.

The Catholic clergy were also more in favor of applying Christian principles to social and political issues and movements. It would seem that the Catholic clergy think of the Church as providing the theological grounding for protest and political movements, but, as we mentioned before, are hesitant to see the Church commit herself publicly on a given issue. The Church should act as a model and example of Christian principles but refrain from direct interference in political affairs. A good example of this position is the response to the morality of the Vietnam war issue. Far less than the majority (37 percent) were willing to agree with the statement that American involvement in Vietnam has been immoral.

Another important area involving values is personal morality, covering such issues as divorce and abortion. The national survey of the priesthood found that

> . . . there seems little reason to doubt that support among the clergy for the Church's teaching on birth control and divorce is waning, but there is little evidence of a change in position on either pre-marital sex or abortion (Greeley, 1972b:125-126).

This agrees with the findings from our survey. Table 2-9 summarizes the favorable response to various personal moral issues.

It appears from these data that the Catholic clergy from the ten communities surveyed generally uphold the traditions of the Catholic Church in the area of personal morality. There is no slippage in the extra-marital question and little in the pre-marital or abortion issues. The contrast with the other clergy groups is striking. There is, for instance, a difference of over 50 percent in the abortion issue.[13]

There is some hesitancy, however, to declare divorce as wrong, as the national priesthood survey indicated.[14] Nor are the priests willing to consider the moral code as an absolute which is to be enforced without compromise. Only 36 percent felt that a moral code should be strictly enforced. This seems to indicate that the Catholic clergy are willing to give direction and counsel and hold up a moral code of right conduct as a guide, but do not feel obliged to enforce strict conformity to that code. They appear to be willing to allow the individuals to make up their own minds on specific moral issues.

TABLE 2-9

CLERGY AGREEMENT ON PERSONAL MORALITY STATEMENTS, BY PERCENT,
RANKED IN ORDER OF TOTAL AGREEMENT BY THE CATHOLIC CLERGY

| Statement | Catholic Clergy | | | Other Clergy |
	Strongly Agree	Agree	Total Agreement	Total Agreement
1. It is wrong for married people to have sexual relations with persons other than their spouse.	100	0	100	80
2. It is wrong for people to have pre-marital sexual relations.	64	23	87	65
3. It is wrong for a woman who wants an abortion in the first trimester to have one.	73	9	81	30
4. Divorce is wrong.	36	18	54	24
5. The Church should enforce a strict standard of moral conduct among its members.	9	27	36	30

The clergy were also asked in the survey to make judgments regarding the decisions they thought their parishioners would make when
confronted by specific moral issues. Whether or not they judged correctly
will be reserved for the next chapter. What concerns us now is the estimates the clergy made of their parishioners' attitude and feelings.

Clergy Estimates

In estimating their parishioners' feelings, the Catholic clergy
felt that in general, they were well liked by their people. Over 85
percent of them characterized the majority of the parishioners' attitudes

as favorable toward themselves and their work in the parish. Nearly a third (32 percent) said they thought that their parishioners had become even more favorable toward them and their work in recent years. The Catholic clergy, however, said that they had noticed a drop in actual attendance at parish functions and activities by their people over the past few years. Table 2-10 indicates the clergy's appraisal of trends in their parishes.

TABLE 2-10

PERCENTAGE OF CLERGY WHO INDICATED A DECLINE IN VARIOUS
PARISH FUNCTIONS, RANKED IN ORDER OF TOTAL
CATHOLIC CLERGY WHO INDICATED A DECLINE

| Parish Function | Catholic Clergy | | | Other Clergy |
	Definite Decline	Possible Decline	Total Decline	Total Decline
1. Number coming to confession	73	14	87	--
2. Support of the parish school	64	14	78	--
3. Involvement of youth in the parish	59	18	77	39
4. Number coming for advice and counsel	55	14	69	17
5. Involvement of adults in the parish	50	18	68	49
6. Support of renewal attempts in the parish	27	41	68	49
7. Regular Mass (worship) attendance	32	27	59	58

In all instances the majority of the Catholic clergy detected a drop in parish attendance and support. Not as many of the other clergy

groups noticed a drop in parish involvement. But neither have their
churches undergone such a profound change in parish life as have the
Catholic parishes following the Second Vatican Council. The Catholic
clergy are acutely aware of the shift that has occurred in recent years,
and they realize that they can no longer presume that their parishioners
will give unqualified support to their parish schools and parish activities, attend parish liturgies, or come to them seeking help and advice.
In Chapter V we will look at some of the reasons for this shift in religious attitudes and practices among the American Catholic population.
For the present we are more concerned with how the clergy view their
parishioners.

TABLE 2-11

PERCENTAGE OF CATHOLIC CLERGY WHO ESTIMATED THAT THE
MAJORITY OF THE PARISHIONERS WOULD AGREE
WITH THESE MORAL STATEMENTS

Statement	Number of Clergy Who Estimated Majority of the People Would			Catholic Clergy's Own Stance
	Strongly Agree	Agree	Total Agree	Total Agree
1. Extra-marital sexual rela-tions are wrong	82	14	96	100
2. Pre-marital sexual rela-tions are wrong	55	27	82	87
3. Abortion in the first trimester is wrong	55	14	69	81
4. Need for a strict moral code	5	32	37	36
5. Divorce is wrong	14	18	32	54

In the area of personal and social moral attitudes, for instance, how do the clergy judge the attitudes of their people? First, in the area of personal morality the priests are willing to admit to some slippage among the laity compared with their own moral judgments. But they still consider their people as maintaining a high moral standard. Table 2-11 gives the Catholic clergy estimates as compared with their own position on various personal moral issues.

As this table indicates, the Catholic clergy feel the majority of their people are solidly united against sexual relations outside of the marriage contract. But they do see their parishioners beginning to weaken under public opinion favoring abortion. Nor do they think the parishioners are at all convinced about the immorality of divorce or feel the need for enforcing a strict standard of moral conduct. We will see in the next chapter whether these estimates correspond to the laity's own positions.

TABLE 2-12

PERCENTAGE OF CATHOLIC CLERGY WHO ESTIMATED THAT THE
MAJORITY OF THE PARISHIONERS WOULD AGREE
WITH THESE SOCIAL POLITICAL STATEMENTS

Statement	Percentage of Catholic Clergy Who Estimated the Majority Would			Catholic Clergy's Own Stance
	Strongly Agree	Agree	Total Agree	Total Agree
1. Christian principles can provide a basis for protest movements	0	27	27	82
2. Parishes should try to include all races and peoples	0	13	13	77
3. Suburbs should be racially integrated	0	13	13	77
4. American involvement in Vietnam has been immoral	0	9	9	37

In estimating the parishioners' stance on social and political issues, the Catholic clergy considered the majority of their people to be conservative and this in contrast to their own more liberal stance. Table 2-12 summarizes the response of those clergy who thought that their people would react favorably to various social issues.

The striking contrast between the clergy's own positions and their estimation of their people's positions is revealing. In the case of integration, both of the neighborhood and of the parish, only three of the twenty-two respondents felt their parishioners would agree to this measure. Among the Catholic clergy themselves, over three-fourths of them favored this move. The clergy, then, feel there is a great distance between their own social value orientations and those of their people. This may account for some of the discontent among the Catholic clergy that was mentioned earlier.

There is one more area of information that the survey of the Catholic clergy uncovered that is worth commenting upon, i.e., their ecumenical attitudes. We have drawn many comparisons between Catholic and other clergy groups. But how do the Catholics feel toward these other groups?

One of the conclusions from the national survey indicated that, "There is support for ecumenism among the Catholic clergy and considerable involvement in ecumenical activity" (Greeley, 1972b:311). But it also found that the bishops were ". . . more likely than other priests to attend ecumenical gatherings, to have social and work contact with Protestant and Jewish clergy and to be strongly committed to ecumenism" (Greeley, 1972b:118). How does this compare with the ecumenical attitudes of the Catholic parish clergy in this sample?

The first evidence we have is that while the Catholic clergy were not active in extra-parochial activities, the one activity that most of the Catholic clergy participated in was the local ministerial organization. Sixty-eight percent of them mentioned belonging to such a group and they spent an average of three hours or more a month working in the group. This is closer to the bishops' level of ecumenical activity and well above the diocesan priests' level of activity reported in the national survey.[15]

Another indication of ecumenical attitudes among the Catholic clergy was their feelings toward the beliefs and practices of other faith groups. Table 2-13 summarizes the responses of the Catholic clergy toward a representative list of various religious traditions.

TABLE 2-13

CATHOLIC CLERGY'S RESPONSE TO THE QUESTION: "WHAT IS YOUR
FEELING ABOUT THE BELIEFS AND PRACTICES OF THE
FOLLOWING RELIGIOUS GROUPS?", BY PERCENT

Faith Group	Total Favorable	Mixed Feelings and Unfavorable
1. Lutheran	68	18
2. Judaism	64	18
3. Episcopalian	63	22
4. Presbyterian	59	18
5. Methodist	59	23
6. Southern Baptist	13	59
7. Jehovah's Witnesses	9	59
8. Zen Buddhism	4	27

The Catholic clergy were most favorable toward those religious
traditions they felt were most like their own and least favorable toward
those they felt were farthest from their own beliefs. When asked, for
instance, which two religious groups were most like Catholicism, the
Episcopalian and Lutheran faiths were most often mentioned. When asked
which were least like Catholicism, Jehovah's Witnesses and Zen Buddhism
received the most replies. In the case of Zen Buddhism, 68 percent admitted they did not know enough about it to have an opinion one way or
the other.

But the positive response of the Catholic clergy toward other
faith groups was higher than the response from other clergy groups. For
instance, only 15 percent of the fundamentalist-oriented clergy registered favorable responses toward Catholic beliefs and practices, as did
50 percent of the other Protestant clergy. There appears to be a clear
indication from these data that these Catholic clergy have the interests
of ecumenical dialogue at heart and have an open mind toward religious

traditions other than their own. The only exceptions are the Baptists, Jehovah's Witnesses, and Zen Buddhists, the last being a complete mystery to most of the respondents.

One last bit of evidence. When asked about their personal relations with Protestant and Jewish clergymen, all the Catholic clergy said they were personally acquainted with at least a few Protestant ministers, 50 percent of them stating that they knew personally at least nine Protestant clergymen. Seventy-five percent said they knew at least one Jewish rabbi. The ecumenical dialogue seems to be in progress, at least for the area reported in this survey.

Conclusions

What has concerned us in this chapter is the present situation of the American Catholic clergy. The national survey on the priesthood commissioned by the bishops has been a great help. But there were areas the national survey left untouched, i.e., the comparisons with other clergy groups and with a sampling of the parishioners the clergy serve. We have included in our study these comparisons, as well as predictions by the Catholic clergy of how their people feel about specific personal and moral issues.

What has, in fact, been uncovered in this study? This is what appears to have been found:

(1) The Catholic parish clergy are loyal, dedicated servants of the Church, but they are having greater reservations about policy statements coming from diocesan offices.

(2) Most of their time is spent in parish duties, with little time left over for extra-parochial activities or theological reading and reflection.

(3) They are orthodox in their religious, moral, and social orientations, though there does appear to be some fluctuation on personal moral issues, especially with regard to divorce.

(4) They are in favor of change in the Church, many desiring even a faster rate of change than is going on at present. This is especially true for liturgical practices. They are not, in other words, a static, conservative group.

(5)   They no longer are willing to give unqualified support to their parish school but find it, instead, a drag on the parish resources.

(6)   They are still in control of the decision-making power in the parish but can feel this power slipping away from them and into the hands of the lay boards.

(7)   The clergy are aware of a definite drop in parish involvement among their people on all levels of parish life: attendance at liturgies, reception of the sacraments, participation in parish projects and activities.

(8)   Their estimates of their parishioners' personal moral values are close to their own standards. In most cases the percentage difference is under 10 percent.

(9)   In social moral issues, however, the margin between the clergy's own stance and their estimates of their people's stance is alarmingly great. In many cases the percentage differences reach 50 percent.

(10)   The Catholic clergy are not willing to enforce a strict standard of moral conduct on their people but are more willing to give direction and counsel in personal and social moral matters.

(11)   Finally, there is evidence of a trend among the parish clergy toward diversified forms of ministry. While there is little indication of the parish priest leaving the priesthood in large numbers,[16] there is a trend to other types of ministry such as teaching, chaplaincy, and counseling. This tendency toward diversified ministry found among this group of parish clergy may be a response to the changing needs of a more pluralistic Church.

This is what has been learned about the Catholic clergy, thus far, but as the Evaluation Report of the national priesthood study indicated:

> The priest exists for the laity. To the point that he is conceived as a professional person, they are his clients. In a substantial sense they are omnipresent to this clerical life and ministry. So much so, indeed, that it is difficult to think of the priest without reference to the laity. They are such an inevitable and crucial part of the priest's situation that no description or analysis of the priesthood can properly afford to neglect them (Hughes, et al:1973:20).

If we are to understand, then, the present situation of the clergy we must look to the people. For this reason no more will be said about the situation of the clergy until we investigate the attitudes and practices of the Catholic laity. It is to this investigation that we now turn.

CHAPTER III

THE REALITY:

REACTION OF THE LAITY TO THEIR PARISH

Having looked at the norm, i.e., the emphases and opinions of
the parish clergy, the next step is to learn how these compare with the
attitudes and practices of the parishioners. The analysis of the parishioners' responses will be treated in two parts: Chapter III will consider the parishioners' attitudes toward and identification with the
institutional Church and their association with the local parish. Chapter
IV will deal with the parishioners' own religious, personal, and social
value orientations and how these values are related to Church identification and parish involvement.

The Laity and the Church

What is the laity's relationship to the Church in the years
following the Second Vatican Council? One way of finding an answer was
to ask them how they felt about Catholic beliefs and practices. The
response, like that of the clergy, was very positive. Forty-three percent of the parishioners were highly favorable toward the Catholic faith
and another 34 percent were favorable. In other words, 77 percent of the
people reacted favorably toward the Church. Almost all of the remaining
23 percent said they had mixed feelings about the faith or chose not to
respond to the question. Only 2 percent registered any unfavorable opinions.

But the direct question is not always the best measure of feelings
toward the Church. A better indicator might be to learn how the people
reacted to the changes that have taken place in the Church since the
Second Vatican Council. Table 3-1 gives the people's reaction to these
changes and how their reaction compared with the attitudes of the clergy.

37

TABLE 3-1

RESPONSES OF THE CATHOLIC CLERGY AND LAITY TO THE
QUESTION: "WHAT IS YOUR ATTITUDE TOWARD CHANGES
IN THE AMERICAN CATHOLIC CHURCH?" BY PERCENT

Response	Clergy	Laity	Percentage Difference
1. I was satisfied with the pre-Vatican II Church.	0	16	-16*
2. I would like a slower rate of change	18	8	10
3. I am satisfied with the Church's present rate of change.	36	34	2
4. I look forward to a more rapid rate of change.	18	9	9
5. I feel radical change is necessary in the Church.	23	8	15
6. I am confused and uncertain about changes in the Church.	5	18	-13
7. Other or no opinion.	0	7	--
Total	100	100	

*The minus sign indicates that the response of the laity is greater than the clergy's response.

It is clear from this table that the clergy were more in favor of the changes in the Church than were their parishioners. And yet, despite the differences, the majority of the people (51 percent) were either in favor of the present direction of the Church or looked forward to even greater change.

Still the gap between the laity and the clergy does reveal an area of tension in the parish. Although 41 percent of the clergy desired more change, only 17 percent of the people shared this desire.

Table 3-1 also shows that nearly a fifth of the people did not know what to make of the changes and were left in the state of confusion. Combine this group of confused Catholics with those who were not in favor of the changes and it reveals a sizeable minority in the Church (42 percent) who have difficulties with renewal attempts in the Church. We are beginning to get some insight into the problems of Church identity among her people.

Another indication of Church identity is the people's relationship to their local parish. Although the sole criterion for membership in the Catholic Church is baptism, and people are free to attend whichever Catholic Church they wish,[1] still Catholics have always been urged to attend the geographical parish within whose boundaries they live. Exceptions were made for ethnic parishes which drew from particular nationalities instead of from a geographical area. But for the general rule, identification with the Church was synonymous with belonging to the local parish. It is because of this tradition that the next step in looking at shifting patterns of Church identification deals with the parishioners' relationship to their parish.

Joseph Fichter, S.J. pointed out in his study of parish life in the 1950's that one criterion of identification with the parish is Mass attendance.

Mass attendance may be accepted as the principle external criterion of Catholicism. If a person goes to Mass on Sunday he is at least giving outward adherence to the Catholic Church (Fichter, 1951:152).

This criterion must be used with some caution today since it no longer carries the weight it did at the time of the Fichter study.[2] But it is a good place to begin the study of parish involvement.

A Gallup Poll taken at the same time as this survey showed that only 62 percent of the Catholics who responded attended Church once a week or more (Gallup, 1971:Table 3). In our sample 68 percent of the parishioners attended at least weekly Mass. This is a slightly higher percentage, perhaps because the Gallup survey included in its sample non-parish members. In the sample of Catholic college students ranging from the ages of seventeen to twenty-four, taken at the same time, only 50 percent of them attended Mass on a regular basis. If the parish and college samples were combined the outcome would be closer to the national average.[3]

TABLE 3-2

PARISH MEMBERSHIP BY AGE, IN PERCENT

	Age			
Membership	Under 25	25-34	35-54	55 and Over
Nuclear	0	8	15	12
Modal	65	53	61	70
Marginal	22	15	12	9
Nominal	13	24	12	9
Total	100	100	100	100

Note: x^2 = 24.1   df = 9   p = 0.004   gamma = -0.24

TABLE 3-3

PARISH MEMBERSHIP BY SOCIOECONOMIC STATUS, IN PERCENT

	Status		
Membership	High	Medium	Low
Nuclear	20	12	4
Modal	63	60	60
Marginal	6	12	20
Nominal	11	16	16
Total	100	100	100

Note: x^2 = 22.5   df = 6   p = 0.001   gamma = +0.27

But this gives only the minimum criterion of parish identification
Mass attendance must be combined with other aspects of parish involvement in order to gain a more complete idea of a person's relationship to
the parish and to the Church.

It was possible to construct a measure of parish involvement by
combining Mass attendance with the level of a person's voluntary commit-
ment to parish activities and organizations.[4]

The levels of involvement in the parish were divided into four
groups: the nuclear members were those who not only went to Mass at
least once a week but also took part in at least two other Church functions or activities, the modal members were those who fulfilled their
weekly Mass attendance obligation but were not involved in more than
one parish activity, the marginal members were those for whom Mass
attendance was somewhat sporadic, occurring on an average of once or
twice a month or less, and the nominal members were those who attended
Mass only a few times a year and did not take part in parish activities.[5]
Tables 3-2 and 3-3 give the results of the age and socioeconomic status
breakdowns for these four categories of parish membership.

It is evident from the high correlation of age and status with
parish membership that the younger age and lower status groups tend to
be nearer the border of Church membership. These are not surprising
results. Joseph Fichter's study conducted twenty years ago showed the
same relationship between the younger age groups and less parish involvement (Fichter, 1954:85-86). But it is surprising that the overall
percentage of marginal and nominal Catholics among those who consider
themselves parish members is so high (28 percent). This is the group
that does not fulfill the minimum requirement of weekly Mass attendance.

But the data from these tables do not tell us whether or not
membership patterns are changing. Is there a shift in parish membership
since Vatican II or has this distribution of membership from nuclear to
nominal always been the case? In search of an answer, an Index of Parish
Participation Trends was devised.[6] This index summarized the responses
to questions that asked the parishioners to compare their Mass attendance, size of contributions to the parish, and degree of participation
in parish activities five years ago with their present level of involvement in the parish. The results of the Index of Parish Involvement
Trends showed that 71 percent of the parishioners said they either were
more active in the parish at the time of the survey or had not changed
their level of involvement in recent years. Nineteen percent said they
were less active now and another 9 percent said they were much less active
now than they were five years previously. This gives an overall drop in
parish involvement of 28 percent.

Tables 3-4 and 3-5 show the age and status distributions for Parish Involvement Trends.

TABLE 3-4

INDEX OF PARISH INVOLVEMENT TRENDS BY AGE, IN PERCENT

Membership Trends	Age			
	Under 25	25-34	35-54	55 and Over
Same or greater parish involvement	65	67	74	74
Less or much less parish involvement	35	33	26	26
Total	100	100	100	100

Note: $x^2 = 19.0$ df = 9   p = 0.025   gamma = -0.107

TABLE 3-5

INDEX OF PARISH INVOLVEMENT TRENDS BY
SOCIOECONOMIC STATUS, IN PERCENT

Membership Trends	Status		
	High	Medium	Low
Same or greater parish involvement	72	76	62
Less or much less parish involvement	28	24	38
Total	100	100	100

Note: $x^2 = 11.3$ df = 6   p = 0.08   gamma = +0.077

As can be seen from these tables, the trend toward less parish involvement is evident on all status and age levels. Somewhat greater drops appear in the younger age and lower status groups. Over one-third of these groups indicated less involvement at the time of the survey than previously, and this by their own admission. This substantiates the responses of the Catholic clergy who noticed the drop in Mass attendance and parish involvement over the last few years mentioned in the last chapter.[7]

Rather than relying on external practice, however, it seems appropriate to ask the people about their own attitudes toward specific aspects of parish life in order to gain a better understanding of why there is a decline in parish involvement and Mass attendance.

To this end the people were asked questions about their attitudes toward parish liturgical functions and whether they ever felt uncomfortable in church. Over half of the respondents (53 percent) admitted that they occasionally did feel uncomfortable or uneasy in church. Table 3-6 gives the most frequently mentioned reasons for the discomfort.

TABLE 3-6

PERCENTAGE OF THE CATHOLIC LAITY WHO SAID THEY FELT
UNCOMFORTABLE IN CHURCH FOR THE REASONS GIVEN

Reason for Discomfort	Response
1. Changes in the Church	26
2. What the priests do	13
3. Religious doubts	9
4. Out-moded liturgies	7

This table indicates that the most frequently mentioned reason was the changes that have taken place in liturgical functions over the past few years. Since over a quarter of the people so responded, this area of discomfort deserves more attention. What relation, for instance, exists between this experience of discomfort because of changes in the

liturgy and the decline in parish involvement by the parishioners?
Table 3-7 gives this relationship.

TABLE 3-7

PARISH INVOLVEMENT TRENDS VERSUS DISCOMFORT
DUE TO CHANGES, BY PERCENT

Involvement Trends	No Discomfort	Discomfort
1. Same or greater parish involvement	76	62
2. Less or much less parish involvement	24	38
Total	100	100

Note: $x^2 = 9.5$ df = 1   p = 0.002   gamma = +0.32

The table shows a high correlation between parish involvement
trends and discomfort over the changes. This suggests that one reason
for a drop in attendance at Mass and participation in parish activities
is a disenchantment with the innovations taking place in parish liturgies.

The next step in the process of understanding the parishioners'
shifting response to the parish is to discover, if possible, just which
changes caused the greatest discomfort for the majority of the people.
Table 3-8 provides some indication of how the parishioners reacted to
various liturgical functions and how their attitudes compared with the
clergy's response. They are ranked in order of lay preference.

The percentage differences between the clergy and the parishioners
is revealing. They show a spread of almost 45 percent in the case of
laymen distributing Communion and of almost 40 percent in the cases of
Home Masses and the "Kiss-of-Peace." There is clearly a difference of
liturgical tastes between the two groups. Table 3-8 also shows an interesting mixture of reactions toward liturgical functions by the laity.
Traditional practices such as Benediction and Evening Devotions are
immediately followed by newer liturgical forms such as guitar Masses with
contemporary songs and communal penance services. Further down the list
two contrasting kinds of liturgical practices, the "Kiss-of-Peace" and

TABLE 3-8

CLERGY'S AND LAITY'S FAVORABLE RESPONSE TOWARD VARIOUS
LITURGICAL ACTIVITIES, BY PERCENT

Liturgical Activity	Laity	Clergy	Percent Difference
1. Participation Mass with singing	74	96	22
2. Benedictions and Evening Devotions	70	41	-29*
3. Guitar Mass with contemporary songs	56	82	26
4. Communal penance services	47	68	21
5. Prayer groups and services	47	73	26
6. Baptism during Mass	38	59	21
7. Mass with no singing but with responses	36	41	5
8. Informal Masses in homes	34	73	39
9. The "Kiss-of-Peace" in Mass	26	64	38
10. Quiet Mass with no responses	26	9	-17
11. Laymen distributing Communion	24	68	44
12. Laymen receiving Communion in the hand	20	50	30

*The minus sign indicates that the laity's response is greater than the Clergy's response.

"No-participation Masses", received an equal percentage of favorable responses, both being favored by only a fourth of the people.

This may provide some clue as to why people feel uncomfortable in church and choose to remain absent from parish Masses and activities.

It is not simply a result of new liturgies or old but a more complex reaction coming from different segments of the parish population. Some
parishioners react against the traditional liturgies because they feel
they are outmoded and no longer an adequate form of worship for them.
Others, the more traditional parishioners, reject the innovative attempts
at liturgy because it seems to them that the respect and mystery that
once surrounded the "Latin Mass" are being compromised by the newer,
participative liturgies. The result, discomfort and withdrawal by individuals who feel quite differently toward renewal and liturgical changes.

And yet, despite the discomfort some feel as a result of various
liturgical forms, the majority of the parishioners did say they had had
an experience of prayer and worship as a result of the changes. When
asked to respond to the statement, "Changes in the Mass make it harder
for me to worship", 59 percent rejected this statement. This suggests
that the changes have had a positive influence on the parishioners'
spiritual lives.

Since this question of liturgical reform is so important for
understanding the direction the Catholic parish will take in the future,
it may prove helpful to see how the different age and status groups react to these liturgical functions, and to discover what relationship, if
any, exists between attitudes toward various liturgical activities and
parish involvement trends. An Index of Liturgical Attitudes was constructed in which the liturgical functions were grouped along a continuum
ranging from the more traditional liturgical forms, such as non-participation Masses, to the more progressive forms, such as laymen receiving
Communion in the hand. The Index's distribution by age and status is
given in Tables 3-9 and 3-10.

These tables give some indication that the younger age groups
tend more toward the innovative forms of liturgical activity. This is
to be expected. They also show that among the higher and middle status
groups, which include the higher educational and occupational levels,
there is a tendency toward more innovative liturgical activities.

But does this liturgical index tell us about the people's relationship to the parish and involvement in the parish? There are some
clues. It is possible, for instance, to match the parishioners' liturgical attitudes with shifts in parish involvement. Table 3-11 gives this
relationship.

The relation is not strong but there is some indication that those
with traditional liturgical tastes tend more than any other group to be
less involved in the parish than previously. Perhaps they experience the

gap between their own liturgical preferences and the more progressive
attitudes of their clergy.

TABLE 3-9

THE INDEX OF LITURGICAL ATTITUDES BY AGE, IN PERCENT

Liturgical Attitudes	Age			
	Under 25	25-34	35-54	55 and Over
1. Traditional	5	8	8	8
2. Status quo	54	55	66	72
3. Progressive	41	37	26	20
Total	100	100	100	100

Note: $X^2 = 11.3$ df = 6   p = 0.08   gamma = -0.20

TABLE 3-10

THE INDEX OF LITURGICAL ATTITUDES BY
SOCIOECONOMIC STATUS, IN PERCENT

Liturgical Attitudes	Status		
	High	Medium	Low
1. Traditional	9	7	7
2. Status quo	60	61	71
3. Progressive	31	32	22
Total	100	100	100

Note: $X^2 = 3.75$ df = 4   p = 0.44   gamma = -0.07

TABLE 3-11

LITURGICAL ATTITUDES VERSUS PARISH INVOLVEMENT TRENDS, BY PERCENT

	Liturgical Attitudes		
Involvement Trends	Traditional	Status Quo	Progressive
1. Same or greater parish involvement	65	72	73
2. Less or much less parish involvement	35	28	27
Total	100	100	100

Note: x^2 = 1.14   df = 2   p = 0.57   gamma = -0.06

It is interesting to note that while all three groups of liturgical preference shown in Table 3-11 have significant numbers who are withdrawing their support from the parish, these people do not seem to be going to other churches or worship services. Of the 20 percent who said they occasionally go to other churches and liturgies for various reasons --convenience, vacations, work, etc.--only 4 percent said they attend another church because they dislike their own parish liturgies and only 1 percent said they attend another church because they do not like their own parish priests or activities. It appears from these data that the parishioners who choose to stay away from their parish church, stay away from Church altogether.

Another important indicator of the parishioners' identification with the parish and the Church is their reaction toward various parish activities. Table 3-12 gives the percentage of both the parishioners' and clergy's favorable response to a list of parish functions.

Some important lay-clergy contrasts become apparent from this table. First, both groups appear to be split in their reaction to prayer and devotional groups. Only half of the clergy and the people were favorable toward such activities. Both groups also have an equally low percentage of respondents who are in favor of parish personal growth groups or the parish school.

TABLE 3-12

COMPARISON OF THE CLERGY'S AND LAITY'S FAVORABLE RESPONSE
TO VARIOUS PARISH ACTIVITIES, BY PERCENT

Parish Activity	Laity	Clergy	Percentage Difference
1. Recreational groups	75	59	-16*
2. Fund-raising groups	72	23	-49
3. Liturgical groups	70	91	21
4. Parish service groups	66	55	-11
5. Administrative groups	62	82	20
6. Adult religious education	62	96	34
7. Prayer and devotional groups	49	50	1
8. Social action groups	29	55	26
9. Parish school	29	36	7
10. Experimental personal growth groups	25	27	2

*The minus sign indicates that the laity favorable response was higher than the clergy's response.

It is suspected that the reason for the disfavor toward personal growth groups found among the people is the same reason given for the clergy disfavor. These are new and, for the most part, untried activities in parish life, and people are not at all sure what they entail or what part they play in the parish community.

The low favorable response toward the parish school is worth commenting upon. Only two of the three parishes surveyed had parochial schools attached to the parish, and the school in the lower status parish was over 50 percent black. As a result, the response in Table 3-12 needs qualification. Breaking down the favorable response for each parish, it turns out that 46 percent of the people in the more affluent, upper status parish were in favor of the parish school and 32 percent of the people in the lower status, ethnically-changing parish were in favor of their school. This brings the lay favorable response closer to the clergy's own response. But even with this added qualification, only a minority of the Catholic parishioners are supportive of the parochial school system. This may indicate why the Catholic schools are experiencing a financial crisis. The majority of the people are no longer in favor of the parish schools. This may be the reason 64 percent of the clergy said they noticed a lack of support by the laity for the parish school.

Table 3-12 on favorable attitudes toward parish activities also indicates a great discrepancy between the clergy and lay attitudes toward adult religious education and social action groups. In each of these cases the clergy were approximately 30 percent more in favor of such activities than were the laity. In the case of fund-raising, however, the laity were more in favor of such activities than were the clergy, 50 percent more favorable! A few comments about these discrepancies are in order.

First, fund-raising activities. We have noted in the previous chapter that one possible reason why the clergy were not in favor of such activities is that the responsibility falls on their shoulders for the maintenance and support of the parish. The people, on the other hand, enjoy the socializing and light-hearted character of bazaars, bake sales, and bingo.

As for the attitudes toward adult religious education, the people, though not as universally as the clergy, were in favor of such programs by nearly a two-thirds majority. This is a hopeful sign. But how many parishioners actually participate in such programs is another matter. Only 4 percent of the respondents admitted taking part in adult education programs in the parish.

The response of the laity toward parish social action shows that only a minority of the people are in favor of such activities. Less than a third responded favorably to these activities. Only 1 percent of the parishioners acknowledged being members of social action groups in the parish, but this is probably because the parishes themselves did not have any formal organizations in this area. The attitudes of the laity toward social action involvement and the role of the local parish regarding social issues will be discussed at greater length in the next chapter.

One last area of comparison between the clergy and the lay attitudes toward parish organizations involves their reactions to administrative groups. Table 3-12 shows that the clergy's favorable response
is 20 percent greater than the laity's. A few reflections on this percentage difference: First, it must be noted that the majority of both
the clergy and the laity are in favor of such activities. Secondly,
although the interviews of the clergy showed some mixed feelings, the
priests are willing to share the decision-making powers in the parish
through parish boards, councils, and committees. Thirdly, despite
numerous parish administrative groups, the pastor still exercises ultimate control over the decision-making process in the parish. For instance, when the clergy were asked about the extent of lay participation
in the policy planning of the parish, not one pastor indicated that the
laity of his parish had full powers for initiating policy in all areas
of parish life. Sixty percent of the Protestant and Jewish clergy said
that their laity did have such powers. Half of the Catholic pastors
indicated that the laity had power for initiating policies in at least
some areas. This may indicate that the power structure of the parish is
changing. Four of the ten Catholic pastors also reported having serious
disagreements over policy with their lay boards, and in one case the
board was dissolved over such disagreements. This may shed some light
on the less favorable attitudes expressed by the laity toward administrative groups.

We have been considering various aspects of the parishioners'
attitudes toward and involvement in parish life. Perhaps we should ask
the people directly how they feel. Table 3-13 gives their response on
how they feel toward the local parish as compared with the response of
a corresponding Protestant sample.

The discrepancy between the Catholic and Protestant attitudes
toward their local parish can be explained by their different approaches
to parish membership. The Protestant tradition stresses voluntary association with a parish or congregation. Individuals are free to declare
their association with any local congregation they feel fulfills their
religious aspirations and expectations. The Catholic approach toward
membership in the parish is quite different. (Although, as we will see
in Chapter V, Catholics too are stressing more the voluntary nature of
their relationship to the parish.) But traditionally, Catholics belong
to the Catholic Church and fulfill their obligations to this Church
through the local parish, by attending Masses and receiving the sacraments there. For this reason their attitudes toward the local parish
may vary as their expectations of what the Catholic Church should hold
and teach are communicated to them through the local parish and their
clergy.

TABLE 3-13

CATHOLIC AND PROTESTANT LAITY RESPONSE TO THE QUESTION
"WHAT IS YOUR PRESENT GENERAL ATTITUDE TOWARD
THE LOCAL PARISH?" BY PERCENT

Response	Catholic	Protestant
1. Favorable	57	72
2. Mixed feelings	27	17
3. Unfavorable	8	4
4. No opinion	8	7
Total	100	100

While this may explain some of the differences in opinion between
the Catholic and Protestant reactions to the local parish, still it is
revealing that only 57 percent of the Catholics were favorable toward
their parish. This leaves over a third of the parishioners with mixed
or unfavorable opinions toward the parish.

One last area of comparison may provide us with some clues as to
why Catholics expressed disfavor toward their parish. In the beginning
of this chapter we looked at the people's attitudes toward changes in
the Church as one measure of how they felt about the post-Vatican II
Church. We then looked at the people's involvement in parish life and
how the level of this involvement has changed over the last few years.
It might prove interesting to relate these two responses in order to
discover which groups of people tend to be less involved in parish life
at the present time. Are they those who think the Church is moving too
fast, those who are satisfied with the present rate of change, or those
who look for a more rapid rate of change in the Church? Such information
will give us some idea of why people are not in favor of their parish or
of the Church and how their feelings are carried into action in their
withdrawal from parish involvement. Table 3-14 gives this relationship.

It appears from this table that those who are satisfied with the
present rate of change in the Church are more willing to become involved

TABLE 3-14

ATTITUDES TOWARD CHANGES IN THE CHURCH VERSUS PARISH
INVOLVEMENT TRENDS, BY PERCENT

	Attitudes Toward Changes			
Parish Involvement	Too Fast	Confused	Satisfied	Too Slow
1. Same or more parish involvement	66	63	86	63
2. Less or much less parish involvement	34	37	14	37
Total	100	100	100	100

Note: $X^2 = 28$ df = 3   p = 0.0   gamma = -0.10

in the parish and are more favo ble toward it than is any other group.
Over a third of each of the other groups are withdrawing their support
of the parish. This confirms the results from the data on liturgical
attitudes. Both the traditionalists and the progressives are pulling
back from becoming identified with the parish, as are those who are confused by the changes in the Church. But the withdrawal is for different reasons. The traditionalists feel the Church is moving too fast, and
the parish, which is the place they experience the Church, no longer
corresponds to their own religious desires and expectations. The progressives, on the other hand, feel the Church is not moving fast enough.
The world has passed the Church by while it continues to cling to the
past. They find the parish reflects these same out-dated and antiquated
ideas. Those who are confused simply feel left out and find the Church
insensitive toward their problems of adjusting to change. What can be
done about this situation will be the subject of succeeding chapters.

But the Catholic faith entails more than Mass attendance and
parish involvement. It also involves the living out of the precepts which
the Church teaches. It means carrying the message of the Gospels into
one's daily life. In other words, it is a matter of internalizing the
Christian ideals that the Catholic religion holds up as the norm for each
of her members. Do, in fact, the post-Vatican II Catholics reflect in

their daily lives and in their attitudes the Christian ideals of
prayer, faith, and love? It is to the investigation of these more
personal aspects of the Catholic lay response that we now turn.

CHAPTER IV

THE CARRY-OVER:

THE PARISH IN THE LIVES OF THE PEOPLE

This second half of the study of the Catholic laity deals with
the internalization of the Church's teachings and doctrines. It will
attempt to discover the extent to which Catholics make their own the
ideals and values of the Catholic religion. We are now heading into a
subtle and difficult area of Catholic identification with the Church that
does not deal with external observances but with internal motivations and
value orientations.

We will begin with the laity's prayer life and faith experience.
The Gallup Poll of Catholic opinion, conducted at the same time as this
survey, found that 80 percent of those polled felt that religion played
an important role in their lives (Gallup, 1971: Table 1). Our analysis
will look into how this role of religion is manifested in the individual's
personal experiences and feelings.

For instance, the parishioners were asked, "As an adult have you
ever had an experience of the Presence of God?" Table 4-1 gives the
Catholics' response to this question as compared with the Catholic clergy
and Protestant lay responses.

This table shows that the majority of the Catholic laity do have
a sense of God's presence in their lives and only 11 percent rule out
the experience altogether. They also appear to compare favorably with
the Protestant laity whose tradition puts more stress on the subjective
experiences of religion. Nor do their experiences lag far behind the
Catholic clergy's whose task it is to encourage religious sentiments in
the lives of their people.

It may prove interesting to see how this experience of the presence of God is related to the people's association with the parish.

TABLE 4-1

LAY AND CLERGY RESPONSES TO THE QUESTION, "AS AN ADULT HAVE YOU EVER
HAD AN EXPERIENCE OF THE PRESENCE OF GOD?" BY PERCENT

	Catholic		Protestant
Response	Clergy	Laity	Laity
1. I am sure I have.	36	32	31
2. I think I have.	36	25	30
3. I don't think so.	14	28	27
4. I am sure I have not.	0	11	9
5. No response	13	4	3
Total	99	100	100

Are the people who are most active in the parish the ones who also indicated a sense of God's presence in their lives? Table 4-2 gives this
relationship.

It is obvious from this table that there is a relationship between
the level of involvement in the parish and a person's experience of God's
presence. It does not tell us, however, just how a person's association
with the parish affects his actions and attitudes beyond the general
awareness of God's presence. Does parish involvement and church attendance affect other aspects of a person's life as well?

One indication of the carry-over from the Church to daily life is
the level of religious activity exercised by Catholics in their home.
Judging from the response related to this area of religious activity, it
appears that less than half of the parishioners have any kind of family
prayer or religious discussion in their homes. Only 49 percent even
admitted saying grace before meals. Nor were these families likely to
have prayers outside of mealtime. Less than a quarter of the replies
(24 percent) responded positively to this practice of family prayer. It
is even less likely that scripture reading or any other kind of religious

TABLE 4-2

PARISH MEMBERSHIP AND THE PERSONAL EXPERIENCE
OF GOD'S PRESENCE, BY PERCENT

Experience of God's Presence	Parish Membership			
	Nuclear	Modal	Marginal	Nominal
1. I am sure I have, or I think I have.	74	62	56	37
2. I don't think so, or I am sure I have not.	26	38	44	63
Total	100	100	100	100

Note: $X^2 = 16.2$ df = 3   p = 0.001   gamma = +0.27

reading is going on among these Catholic families. Only 7 percent said that any of these practices had ever been initiated in their homes.

These results, however, come as no surprise to those raised in Catholic homes. The traditional center of religious activity for Catholics has always been the parish, where they gathered for Mass, Confession, and religious devotions. It is only within the past few years that scripture study groups, adult religious education, and informal prayer and liturgy gatherings have broadened the scope of religious activity for Catholics.

Granted that the prayer life of Catholic families is limited--at least in its external manifestations--still it is noteworthy that 42 percent of the respondents said that they discussed the meaning of their faith in their homes at least once or twice a month. Also, over half of the respondents (56 percent) said that the Church and parish had definitely been a help to them through sermons, study groups, counseling, etc., in their personal prayer life. At least there is this much carry-over from the Church to the home.

One indication of how much help the people did receive was the degree to which the laity reflected the teachings of the Catholic Church regarding Christ and the Scripture. The parishioners were asked to respond to the statement, "Jesus Christ is the necessary foundation for my religious faith." They were also asked what was their understanding of the Bible.

In response to the question of the role Christ played in their faith life, 85 percent agreed that he was the foundation of their faith, over half of them (53 percent) expressing strong feelings in this regard. But the response was neither unanimous nor enthusiastic, indicating the struggle between Christian and secular humanistic values in the people's lives.

TABLE 4-3

CLERGY AND LAY ATTITUDES TOWARD SCRIPTURE, BY PERCENT

Response	Clergy	Laity
1. Scripture is literally true.	0	10
2. It is not literally true but is the most important way to God.	37	20
3. It is one of many equally important ways to God.	45	55
4. It is less important than other ways to God.	0	5
5. Other or no opinions.	18	10
Total	100	100

In their understanding of the Bible, the orthodox Catholic teaching was upheld. Table 4-3 shows the clergy-lay comparisons in response to this question regarding their understanding of the Bible.

It appears from this table that the people followed closely the clergy's lead in their understanding of the Bible's place in their religious experience. Seventy-five percent of the lay respondents felt the Bible was not literally true but was one of many ways of knowing about God. This is the orthodox Catholic position which considers sacred tradition, the Mass, and the sacraments as among the many avenues to God's presence and knowledge about Him, in addition to the Scripture.

It is interesting to note how these responses concerning Christ and the Bible related to the level of one's parish involvement. Can we say, for instance, that the more active the parishioner the more orthodox his belief patterns? This seems to be a safe statement since, in the case of the Bible, a greater percentage of the nuclear members did share the orthodox positions of the Church than did the marginal or nominal members. These latter groups tended more toward the position that Scripture was not as important as other ways toward knowing about God. The same was true for the people's understanding of Christ as the foundation of their faith, as Table 4-4 indicates.

TABLE 4-4

JESUS AS THE FOUNDATION OF ONE'S FAITH AND
CHURCH MEMBERSHIP, BY PERCENT

| | Parish Membership | | | |
Jesus as Foundation	Nuclear	Modal	Marginal	Nominal
1. Agreement	92	93	83	80
2. Mixed feelings or disagreement	8	7	17	20
Total	100	100	100	100

Note: $x^2 = 13.3$ df = 3   p = 0.006   gamma = +0.34

This table shows a slight tendency on the part of those who are not actively involved in the parish to be less accepting of Jesus as the foundation of their faith. But, despite this tendency, the great majority of all parish groups are willing to acknowledge Jesus as their Lord.

The Catholic laity were also willing to acknowledge that the Church had a role in the formation of their religious beliefs. Seventy percent said that the Church was helpful, through sermons, study groups,

counseling, etc., in giving them guidance in the formation of their religious beliefs and practices. With the emphasis in the American Catholic Church on a parochial school system this would not seem to be a
surprising response.

But the real test of the degree to which the people's religious
affiliation finds its way into their everyday lives is their attitudes
on personal and social moral value issues. Do the parishioners' personal and social moral attitudes reflect the teachings of the Catholic
Church in these areas?

In search of an answer we will look at the parishioners' reactions to various value statements. We will begin with personal moral
values. Four moral issues will be considered: pre-marital sex, extra-
marital sex (relations with someone other than one's wife or husband),
abortion, and divorce.[1]

We have already considered (in Chapter II) the clergy's stance
on these same moral issues. Their position will serve as the Church's
position on these issues for it is at the parish level of the Church's
authority structure that the people encounter the Church's position most
directly.

We will look at the parishioners' response on these issues and
compare it with the clergy's response in order to understand the degree
to which the Church's stance is reflected in the people's moral attitudes. A table of comparison has been constructed, Table 4-5, which
gives the laity's and clergy's positive response to the four moral value
statements. Also given are the percentage differences between the two
groups.

In each case, the people were not as willing to agree with the
statements as were the clergy, and this by a large margin. The clergy
themselves anticipated this lower response in their estimates of the
parishioners' response to these statements (See Chapter II, Table 2-11).
Almost all of the clergy thought the majority of their people would consider extra-marital and pre-marital sexual relations to be wrong. Their
judgment was correct since the majority of the people did so respond.
But it was a bare majority (51 percent) in the case of pre-marital sex.

The clergy were also accurate in estimating that the majority of
their parishioners would not consider divorce as wrong. A large percentage of the people (29 percent) considered that the circumstances
surrounding divorce made a difference, and another 20 percent said they
had mixed feelings about its morality. The clergy predicted this response

TABLE 4-5

COMPARISON OF THE CLERGY AND LAITY FAVORABLE RESPONSE
TO PERSONAL MORAL VALUE STATEMENTS, BY PERCENT

	Percentage Who Agreed with the Statement		
Moral Value Statements	Clergy	Laity	Percentage Difference
1. It is wrong for married people to have sexual relations with persons other than their husbands or wives.	100	80	20
2. It is wrong for people to have pre-marital sexual relations.	87	51	36
3. It is wrong for a woman who wants an abortion in the first trimester to have one.	81	41	40
4. Divorce is wrong.	54	28[a]	26

[a]The findings from the national poll of Catholic opinion support this result. It showed that 28 percent of those polled felt divorce and re-marriage was wrong. (See Gallup, 1971: Table 35.)

since half of them judged their people's response to be circumstantial or ambiguous in reacting to the "divorce-is-wrong" statement.

But the Catholic clergy were not aware of how few of their people would agree with the "abortion-is-wrong" statement. Seventy percent of the clergy felt the majority of the parishioners would consider abortion to be wrong. In reality, only 40 percent of the parishioners did. There appears to be a much greater slippage from the orthodox Catholic position on abortion among the people than the clergy were either aware of or willing to admit.

As in the case of divorce, many Catholics considered abortion an open question. Forty percent of the respondents indicated that they either had mixed feelings about the morality of abortion or that it depended on the circumstances of the case. The Gallup Poll showed similar results. Fifty-eight percent of the people who responded to the Gallup survey said they would be in favor of allowing an abortion in the case of a young girl who became pregnant because she was raped (Gallup, 1971: Table 29).

The positions of the Catholic laity on personal moral issues are, in fact, closer to the Protestant laity's attitudes. Table 4-6 gives the comparison of Catholic and Protestant favorable responses to the same four personal moral statements used in the previous table.

TABLE 4-6

COMPARISON OF CATHOLIC AND PROTESTANT LAY FAVORABLE RESPONSES
TO PERSONAL MORAL VALUE STATEMENTS, BY PERCENT

	Percentage Who Agreed with the Statement		
Moral Value Statements	Catholic	Protestant	Percent Difference
1. Extra-marital sexual relations are wrong.	80	82	− 2*
2. Pre-marital sexual relations are wrong.	51	51	0
3. Abortion in the first trimester is wrong.	41	10	31
4. Divorce is wrong.	28	11	17

*The minus sign indicates the Protestant response is greater than the Catholic response.

There is no difference between the Catholic and Protestant groups in their reaction to sexual relations outside marriage. The reactions, however, toward abortion and divorce do show discrepancies. Many more Catholics consider abortion and divorce to be wrong. But despite the larger percentage of Catholics than Protestants who oppose these actions, still the shift toward a more lenient position by a majority of the Catholics is revealing.

The next question that needs to be asked is how these attitudes relate to the laity's association with the Church and the parish. Is it only the marginal and nominal parish members, for instance, who hold permissive and lenient views on personal moral issues or are these attitudes prevalent on all levels of parish membership and involvement?

In looking for an answer to this question, an Index of Personal Moral Values was constructed which summarized the Catholic laity's response to the four moral issues used in Tables 4-5 and 4-6. This index was then correlated with age, status, Church membership, parish involvement trends, and attitudes toward the local parish and changes in the Church. The results of this analysis showed that, in general, the younger age groups were more inclined toward lenient and circumstantial attitudes on moral issues. The socioeconomic status breakdown, on the other hand, gave little indication that either the higher or lower status groups were more likely to hold circumstantial moral attitudes. From all the data compiled, the following table was selected as being the most representative and interesting since it gives some information about the connection between the laity's position on moral issues and shifts in parish involvement over the last few years. Table 4-7 shows the relationship.

The combined circumstantial and lenient response, when compared with the total Catholic response, came to 41 percent of the parishioners. This represents a sizeable minority of Catholics who feel that actions that are explicitly prohibited by the Church are, at least for them, open questions. They feel, in other words, that actions such as abortion and divorce cannot be universally and automatically labeled as "wrong." And, as Table 4-7 indicates, there is some connection between such feelings and the people's withdrawal from parish involvement.

Can it be said, then, that Catholics consider that a strict moral code is no longer desirable in this modern age of personal decision-making and individual freedom? The answer from the respondents is not clear. The parishioners were asked to react to the statement: "The Church should enforce a strict standard of moral conduct among its members." The response was almost equally divided between agreement (38 percent) and disagreement (31 percent), with the balance either expressing ambiguous feelings (20 percent) or choosing not to respond to the statement (11 percent).

TABLE 4-7

PERSONAL VALUE ORIENTATIONS OF THE CATHOLIC LAITY
AND PARISH INVOLVEMENT TRENDS, BY PERCENT

Parish Involvement	Value Orientations		
	Orthodox	Circumstantial	Lenient
1. Same or greater parish involvement.	76	65	59
2. Less or much less parish involvement.	24	35	41
Total	100	100	100

Note: x^2 = 10.2   df = 2   p = 0.006   gamma = +0.28

         This is almost the identical response that the clergy gave to
the same question. This indicates that there is some reluctance on the
part of the majority of both the clergy and the people to have the Church
enforce a strict code of moral conduct on her people (See Chapter II for
a discussion of clergy reactions to these questions.).

         How do these attitudes toward a moral standard correspond to the
parishioners' identification with the Church and parish involvement? In
order to explore this question, the parishioners' reactions to the need
for a strict moral code were correlated with parish involvement trends
to see which group, those who seek a strict moral code or those who do
not, had the greater proportion of those withdrawing their support of
the parish over the past few years. Table 4-8 gives the results of this
correlation.

         Table 4-8 suggests, though the relationship is not strong, that
those who are looking for a relaxation of the Church's code on personal
moral issues are also those who are more likely to be withdrawing from
parish involvement. There is a connection, then, between more lenient
ideas toward personal morality or a strict moral code and the drop in
parish participation. It is also clear that the moral attitudes of even
the more active parish members lean more toward the general culture mores,

TABLE 4-8

DESIRE FOR A STRICT MORAL CODE VERSUS PARISH
INVOLVEMENT TRENDS, BY PERCENT

	Desire for Moral Code		
Parish Involvement	Desiring Strict Code	Ambiguous Feelings	Not Desiring Strict Code
1. Greater or some parish involvement.	76	80	65
2. Less or much less parish involvement.	24	20	35
Total	100	100	100

Note: x^2 = 8.34   df = 2   p = 0.015   gamma = +0.18

as the comparison with the Protestant laity showed (Table 4-6), than
toward the orthodox positions of the Church, as represented by her clergy
(Table 4-5). If this is the situation in the personal sphere, what can
we expect to find in their attitudes toward social concerns?

To arrive at some idea of the people's attitudes toward social
concerns the same four social issues were used as were used in the
analysis of the clergy's social attitudes. These issues were: integration of the suburbs, opening the parish to all races and social classes,
the morality of the Vietnam war, and the application of Christian principles to social protest movements (See Chapter II). Here again it was
possible to compare the people's position on social values with the
position of the Church by using the opinions of the parish clergy as the
standard. Table 4-9 gives a summary of the results of this comparison,
showing the percentages of the lay respondents who agreed with the statements on the four social issues as compared with the clergy's own response.

As was the case in personal moral issues, the clergy response
ranked higher in agreement with these social value statements than did
their parishioners' response. On the issue of integration of the suburbs,

TABLE 4-9

COMPARISON OF LAITY AND CLERGY FAVORABLE RESPONSE
TO VARIOUS SOCIAL VALUE ISSUES, BY PERCENT

Social Value Statements	Clergy Agreement	Laity Agreement	Percentage Difference
1. Parishes should try to include all races and classes.	77	58	19
2. Suburbs should be racially integrated.	77	35	42
3. Christian principles can provide a basis for protest movements.	82	30	52
4. American involvement in Vietnam has been immoral.	37	28[a]	9

[a]This agrees with the Gallup Poll's findings on attitudes toward the Church taking a stand on the war in Vietnam. In that survey 31 percent agreed with the Church taking a stand. (See Gallup, 1971: Table 35.)

for instance, there was a difference of opinion of 42 percentage points. And, excluding the Vietnam War issue, the difference between lay and clergy responses was, on the average thirty-three percentage points apart.

The clergy suspected this in their estimation of their parishioners' response to this issue of suburban integration. Only three of the clergy (13 percent) thought the majority of the people would agree with this statement (See Chapter II, Table 2-12). Most of the clergy were mistaken, however, in estimating the lay response to the statement on incorporating all races and classes in the parish. Again only three of the clergy felt the majority of their parishioners would agree with this statement. In fact, almost 60 percent of them did agree. It appears, then, that at least in this one instance, the people were more liberally inclined than the clergy gave them credit for. There are various reasons for this more liberal stance toward integration of the parish than of the neighborhood. For one thing the wording of the suburban integration issue was specific, while the parish integration statement included racial and social groups. Then again, people might have had more difficulty excluding a specific group from sharing the Mass with them than from sharing their neighborhood.

Another explanation becomes apparent in looking at the responses from individual parishes. The parishioners from the lower status, more ethnic parish were much more open to an integrated parish than were parishioners from the upper status parish, 67 percent versus 44 percent. One reason is that 15 percent of the respondents from the lower status parish were black. But another reason is that in this parish many people, even though they have moved out of the neighborhood when the blacks moved in, still belong to their old parish and attend Mass there. They have, in other words, had an easier time accepting blacks into the parish than accepting them into their neighborhoods.

The Catholic lay response on social issues was much closer to the Protestant lay response than to the Catholic clergy's. Table 4-10 shows the comparison of the favorable responses from both groups of laity.

TABLE 4-10

PERCENTAGE OF LAY CATHOLIC AND PROTESTANT FAVORABLE
RESPONSE TO SOCIAL VALUE ISSUES

Social Value Statements	Catholic Agree	Protestant Agree	Percentage Difference
1. Integration of the parish.	58	53	5
2. Integration of the suburbs.	35	39	- 4*
3. Christian principles for protest movements.	30	33	- 3
4. Morality of the Vietnam War.	28	23	5

*The minus sign indicates that the Protestant response is greater than the Catholic response.

It appears from these data that, as was the case in personal moral issues, the Catholic laity agree more with the social mores of their Protestant neighbors than with the stance of their parish clergy.

There are other indications of the laity's attitudes toward social issues, especially as these issues are related to the local parish. The parishioners were given a number of choices of how the parish might respond to public policy issues. The choices ranged from the parish taking an official stand on public policy to the complete isolation of the parish from the public sphere. The responses to these choices are summarized in Table 4-11. The clergy's own response is included by way of comparison (See Chapter II for a discussion of the Catholic clergy's reaction to this question.)

The percentage difference in Table 4-11 between the clergy's and the parishioners' reaction is revealing. For instance, although all the parish clergy agreed that at the very least the people in the parish should be encouraged to become involved in non-parish affiliated social activities, less than half of the people felt this way. In fact, nearly a fourth of the parishioners (23 percent) went so far as to say the parish should take no stand whatever on public policy issues.

To put it another way, the line was drawn by the clergy at the parish taking an official stand on public policy issues or agreeing to the formation of parish-sponsored social action groups. The majority of the clergy voted against these measures. But they were in favor of giving encouragement to individuals to become involved in social action on their own or to allow people to discuss the issues informally in the parish. The clergy emphasis, then, was on providing guidance and direction to the people rather than on having the parish itself becoming directly involved.

For the laity, however, the line was drawn much further back from social involvement. Less than half of them (47 percent) were willing to let the parish give support to individuals who become involved in such activity and less than a third (30 percent or less) were willing to let the parish become associated in any way with social action groups, even to the extent of allowing the parish buildings to be used by social action groups.

This feeling was reinforced in the response to the statement: "The American Catholic Church should take public stands on political issues." Sixty percent rejected this statement, almost half of them expressing strong disagreement with this position. This was in contrast to 32 percent of the clergy who agreed with the Church taking a stand on

political issues and 18 percent who were against it. The rest of the
clergy had ambiguous feelings toward the role of the Church in the public
sphere. The majority of the parishioners, however, were more certain of
the political role of the Church, i.e., do not take a stand on such
issues.

TABLE 4-11

COMPARISON OF LAY AND CLERGY RESPONSE TO THE ROLE OF THE
PARISH IN PUBLIC POLICY ISSUES, BY PERCENT

Parish Role in Public Issues	Clergy Agreement	Laity Agreement	Percentage Difference
1. Taking official stands on public policy issues.	36	7	29
2. Encourage people to form un-official parish action groups.	23	17	6
3. Encourage people to form parish discussion groups.	82	28	54
4. Allow parish buildings to be used for social action groups.	73	30	43
5. Encourage people to participate in community action.	100	47	53
6. The parish should take no stand on public policy.	0	23	-23*

*The minus sign indicates that the laity's response is greater
than the clergy's response.

Since there was such a discrepancy between the clergy and the
lay reactions to the involvement of the parish in public policy issues,
it may prove interesting to compare the Catholic lay response with the
Protestant lay response to see what discrepancies existed between these
two groups. Table 4-12 gives this comparison.

The Catholic lay response is, in every case, closer to the Protestant lay response than to the Catholic clergy response. What is worth noticing, however, is that the Protestant parishioners were more open than Catholics to parish members becoming involved in social action, allowing the parish to be used for social actions groups, and to the formation of parish discussion groups in these areas.

TABLE 4-12

COMPARISON OF THE CATHOLIC AND PROTESTANT RESPONSE TO THE ROLE
OF THE PARISH TOWARD PUBLIC POLICY ISSUES, BY PERCENT

Parish Role	Catholic Agreement	Protestant Agreement	Percentage Difference
1. Taking official stands.	7	8	- 1*
2. Encourage unofficial groups.	17	19	- 2
3. Encourage discussion groups.	28	39	-11
4. Allow parish buildings to be used.	30	40	-10
5. Encourage community social activity.	47	56	- 9
6. No parish involvement.	23	16	7

*The minus sign indicates the Protestant response is greater than the Catholic response.

The American Catholic tradition has had a long history of lay involvement in social action. Dorothy Day and her Catholic Worker movement, Catholic involvement in the anti-war movement, and efforts to change the abortion legislation are indications of this involvement. What these present data show is that this tradition of social involvement is composed of and encouraged by a small minority of the Catholic laity. The majority of the people, however, consider public involvement as foreign to their concept of the Church. Neither are they in favor of the Church encouraging people to work for social change. Their concept of the Church seems to be associated more with spiritual concerns and personal salvation.

In order to find out how these attitudes of the Catholic population toward Church involvement in public policy matters are related to attitudes on specific social issues, an Index of Parish Policy Involvement was constructed from the data contained in Tables 4-11 and 4-12. This index was then correlated with the parishioners' attitudes toward integration of the suburbs. Table 4-13 shows the results of this correlation.

TABLE 4-13

PARISH PUBLIC POLICY INVOLVEMENT VERSUS CATHOLIC LAY ATTITUDES
TOWARD INTEGRATION OF THE SUBURBS, BY PERCENT

Attitudes Toward Integration	Level of Parish Public Policy Involvement			
	High	Medium	Low	None
1. Agreement	54	43	32	19
2. Mixed feelings	34	40	42	43
3. Disagreement	12	17	26	38
Total	100	100	100	100

Note: $X^2 = 42.5$ df = 6   p = 0.00   gamma = +0.36

There can be little doubt that those who wish to keep the parish out of the public sphere are the same people who find it most difficult to accept integration in the suburbs. They would rather see the Church dealing solely with spiritual matters and leaving social issues to secular society.

The one exception to this attitude was the Catholic lay response to government aid to parochial schools. The responses of the Catholic and Protestant laity were quite different on this issue. Fifty-six

percent of the Catholics were in favor of such a move while only 15 percent of the Protestants were favorable. This is a 41 percent difference!

To see how Catholic attitudes toward social involvement were related to their feelings about the Church, their reaction to the parish's
role in public policy was compared with their feelings about changes in
the Church. This was done in order to discover whether the people who
were confused or negative toward the changes in the Church were also
those who were against parish social involvement, or whether it was those
in favor of the changes who were against parish social involvement.
Table 4-14 provides some clues as how these groups compare.

TABLE 4-14

PARISH PUBLIC POLICY INVOLVEMENT VERSUS CATHOLIC LAY ATTITUDES
TOWARD CHANGES IN THE CHURCH, BY PERCENT

	Level of Parish Public Policy Involvement			
Attitudes Toward Changes	High	Medium	Low	None
1. Traditional	21	21	23	40
2. Confused	12	17	14	22
3. Status quo	35	39	43	34
4. Progressive	32	23	20	4
Total	100	100	100	100

Note: $x^2 = 40.2$ df = 9   p = 0.0001   gamma = -0.28

As was expected, it was the traditionalists, i.e., those who
felt the Church was changing too fast, who also felt it should stay out
of the public realm. Perhaps they felt the changes in the Church were
taking it into this realm and they were apprehensive of this shift. The
opposite could be said of the group who looked forward to a more rapid
rate of change, i.e., the progressives. Since they were much more open

to social involvement and considered the role of the parish as providing
a voice in social and political areas, it may be just such changes they
hoped would receive a greater emphasis in the Church in the future.

But, judging from the data uncovered in this survey, those seeking a shift toward greater Church involvement in social issues have a
difficult struggle ahead of them because of the strong isolationalist,
non-involvement stance voiced by the majority of the Catholic laity.

To take one example, only 30 percent of the lay respondents
approved of the clergy taking a stand on either school busing or the
Vietnam war, no matter what the clergy's stand may be. In issues connected with welfare recipients or business ethics, less than half of the
respondents (45 percent) approved of their clergy taking a stand on
these issues, again, no matter what the stand. This does seem to
indicate a desire on the part of the majority of the parishioners to
restrict the role of the Church to matters of personal piety and spiritual concerns.

Perhaps the Church itself is at fault as much as the laity in
limiting its sphere of influence in American society. When asked whether
the Church had given them any help in forming social attitudes, only 21
percent of the laity said that they had received help. The majority
(53 percent) said the Church had been of little help one way or another
in giving them direction on social issues. Another 14 percent said the
Church, in fact, had been unhelpful in giving them guidance on social
issues.

We have already seen that 63 percent of the clergy did talk about
social and political issues in their sermons and instructions to the
people (See Chapter II, Table 2-6.) And yet, only 21 percent of the
people felt the Church had been helpful in giving them guidance in these
areas. It appears from this comparison of clergy emphasis and lay reception that the majority of the people would rather not be given guidance by the Church or the clergy in these areas.

One indication of this difficulty of communicating the Church's
teachings on social justice to the people is the discrepancy that seems
to exist between the parishioners' attitudes on integration of the suburbs
and their participation in the parish. Table 4-15 shows the relationship.

The teachings of the Catholic Church have emphasized the ideals
of human dignity and individual rights and have called the American
people to task for their attitudes toward segregation and restrictive
housing.[2] Over three-fourths of the Catholic clergy serving the respon-

dents of this survey were in favor of integration of the suburbs. And yet, as Table 4-15 shows, less than half of the nuclear members of the parish agreed that the suburbs should include all races and peoples. These are the most active parishioners who form the core of the parish. But it is true that the nuclear members were more in favor of suburban integration than any of the other groups. Only 36 to 39 percent of the other groups were in agreement with this issue. This includes the modal members who faithfully attend Mass every week. It would appear from this that church attendance has had little effect on the formation of at least this one social attitude.

TABLE 4-15

PARISH MEMBERSHIP VERSUS CATHOLIC LAY ATTITUDES
ON INTEGRATION OF THE SUBURBS, BY PERCENT

| | Church Membership | | | |
Integration Attitudes	Nuclear	Modal	Marginal	Nominal
1. Agreement	47	36	37	39
2. Mixed feelings	33	41	36	38
3. Disagreement	20	23	27	23
Total	100	100	100	100

Note: $x^2 = 3.83$ df = 6   p = 0.7   gamma = +0.05

We have been investigating the personal and social moral value orientations of a group of Catholic parishioners. There is one more area to look at involving family life. In this case the clergy-lay comparisons will not provide contrasts of lay opinion and the Church's teachings as in the other cases. But they will provide an insight into the differences between clergy and lay approaches to family decision-making and child-rearing practices.

We have already seen that the Catholic clergy's emphasis in family life is toward shared decision-making. (See Chapter II, Table 2-6.)

Table 4-16 shows how their attitudes compared with the laity's in deter-
mining who should make the major decisions in the home.

TABLE 4-16

CLERGY AND LAITY COMPARISONS IN FAMILY
DECISION-MAKING, BY PERCENT

Locus of Decision- Making in the Home	Clergy Agreement	Laity Agreement	Percentage Difference
1. Either the husband or the wife should make decisions.	0	6	- 6*
2. The husband and wife together should make the decisions.	50	69	-19
3. The husband and wife after consulting the children.	32	10	22
4. The family as a whole should make the decisions.	18	10	8
5. Other or no opinion.	0	5	--

*The minus sign indicates that the laity response is greater than
the clergy response.

It appears from this table that the clergy were more willing to
allow the children to enter into the decision-making process than were
the laity. And yet, looking at the responses to the question: "What is
the most important thing for a child to learn to prepare himself for
life?" the highest response from the laity (62 percent) was that the
child should learn to think for himself. Only 50 percent of the clergy
so responded.

This uncovers an interesting mixture of attitudes among the laity;
reserving family decisions to the parents and encouraging independence
among the children. The clergy, on the other hand, were much more in
favor of teaching the children to be aware of and helpful toward those
in need. Twenty-seven percent of the clergy, compared with 14 percent

of the laity, thought this was the most important thing for a child to learn in order to prepare himself for life.

Perhaps this difference in approach toward family decision-making and child-raising is the reason only half of the people felt they had received help from the Church and their clergy in domestic matters. This despite the insistence of 78 percent of the clergy that they had emphasized these subjects in their sermons and teachings.

This discrepancy may be one reason that 47 percent of the parishioners were in favor of a married clergy and another 30 percent had mixed feelings about it. Only 23 percent were definitely against it.[3] Perhaps the people feel that if priests had families of their own they would be in a better position to understand the problems and difficulties facing parents in making family decisions and in raising children.

Having analyzed the data on religious, familial, personal, and social value orientations of a group of Catholic parishioners, what can we now say about the internalization of the Catholic Church's doctrine and teachings by her people? As was mentioned in the beginning of this chapter, our data are limited to parish membership roles and for that reason whatever is said here cannot hope to reflect the values and opinions of the entire Catholic population. But the data do give some idea of the attitudes of at least the people who are identified with the Church to the extent that they consider themselves members of a Catholic parish. This group makes up the majority of the Catholic population. What, then, can be said about this group?

Conclusion

This is what has been uncovered in the last two chapters on the Catholic laity:

(1) There is a sizeable drop in parish involvement over the past few years, a drop of nearly 30 percent. For some it means attending another Church or worship service but for the vast majority it means no church attendance at all.

(2) A large percentage of both traditional and progressive Catholics find it difficult "fitting-in" with the "new" Church. It does not fulfill their needs, varied and diverse as they are.

(3) Catholics are making their own decisions on personal moral

and social moral issues which once were reserved to the authority of the Church. They feel freer to consider their own situation as unique, and they act accordingly. Their position on abortion is one example.

(4) The influence of the Catholic hierarchy, especially as exercised by the parish clergy, is being challenged by the power or the indifference of the laity, i.e., the directives of the Church are being directly confronted or simply ignored by many of her people.

(5) The majority of Catholics feel the Church should stay out of sociopolitical matters and concentrate on more traditional, spiritual concerns.

(6) The Catholic laity's positions on personal and social moral issues follow more closely the value orientations of the general American culture, as represented by the Protestant lay sample, than they do the Church's stance on these matters, as represented by the Catholic clergy.

This, in broad outline, is what the survey of the Catholic laity uncovered. Where it will take the Catholic Church in America is not certain. The change has come swiftly and has been the cause of much confusion and uncertainty among the people. The next step in our investigation of the American Catholic Church and shifting parish membership is to look at some of the causes for the change and the reasons for the confusion and uncertainty that have accompanied the change.

CHAPTER V

THE SHIFT:

SOME REASONS FOR THE CHANGE IN MEMBERSHIP

We have been looking at shifting patterns of membership and
Church identification among a group of American Catholics. The dominant
pattern that is emerging is that Catholics are inclined to make up their
own minds, not only in their involvement in parish life, but in their
value orientations as well. The Church and the parish are still their
guide but not their sole authority. The American Catholic Church, in
other words, is becoming a voluntary Church much like the Protestant
tradition of membership.

The drop in parish involvement, the freedom people feel to attend
Mass or not, the spreading out of parish decision-making to include the
laity, the Catholics' personal and social moral value orientations which
follow cultural rather than religious norms--all these facets of the
current situation point to a more voluntaristic, pluralistic Catholic
religion.

But it is not enough to explain what is happening. The attempt
must also be made to explain why this is happening in the Church at the
present time. It is this question of why there is a shift in Church
membership patterns among Catholics that is the subject of this final
chapter.

We will now attempt, after having gained some knowledge of the
current situation of the American Catholic parish, to offer a few reasons
for the shifting patterns of Church participation and value orientations
that have been discussed in previous chapters. The reasons will be
summarized under three headings: (1) historical, (2) cultural, and (3)
theological. We will begin with the historical.

79

Historical Reasons

The American Catholic Church is an ethnic church. The majority of its people arrived on the scene after the cultural mores had been established. Until quite recently being associated with the Catholic religion carried with it an implied association with a subculture in American society. To be identified as Catholic was to be identified with a group that was along side of, but not entirely part of, the dominant culture.

But American Catholics of the seventies no longer feel apart from the mainstream of American culture because of their religious affiliation. They are not even sure that being a Catholic is that much different from being a Protestant in today's pluralistic society.[1]

As proof of this, the Catholic lay respondents to our survey were almost unanimous (88 percent) in their rejection of the statement: "Being a Catholic makes it harder for me to feel I am part of American society." Only 2 percent agreed with this statement. When asked their feelings toward the statement, "There is no longer much difference between Catholic and Protestant churches," over a third of them (35 percent) agreed and another 27 percent expressed mixed feelings or offered no opinion. The Catholic laity, in fact, were much more willing than were either the Catholic clergy or the Protestant laity to think little of the differences between the Catholic and Protestant faiths. Only 10 percent of the Catholic clergy and 19 percent of the Protestant laity agreed that there was no longer much difference between Catholic and Protestant churches, compared with the 35 percent response of the Catholic laity.

These attitudes among the Catholics seem to indicate that the Catholic ethnic ghetto is a thing of the past. There are still pockets of ethnic consciousness, especially among the Spanish-speaking groups and to a lesser extent, the Eastern European Catholics. But this is largely because they are the most recent Catholic arrivals to the American scene.

The majority of today's American Catholics are native born and do not claim any ethnic identity. In our sample, 85 percent of the Catholic respondents were born in the United States, and when asked: "Do you think of yourself as belonging to a particular nationality or ethnic group?," 67 percent of them claimed no ethnic origin.

This result is in support of Philip Gleason's analysis of the current American Catholic situation. He states:

. . . the Catholic population considered as a whole is no longer
made up of national "hyphenates"--people whose perception of
themselves as Americans was qualified by the awareness that they
belong to distinctive national minorities (Gleason, 1969:8).

This loss of ethnic consciousness and the corresponding identification with the American culture provide clues as to why "Catholic"
organizations, institutions, and schools are finding survival so difficult. Catholics no longer see the need to continue a sub-system of
Catholic social, political, educational, and economic institutions when
they themselves no longer relate to a sub-culture distinct from the
dominant American way of life.

These Catholic organizations were founded in order to provide
outlets for Catholic immigrants at a time when it was impossible or, at
least undesirable, to identify with the existing social, political, and
educational organizations of the predominantly Protestant culture. The
prohibition by the Church against Catholic participation in the YMCA or
YWCA, for example, continued into the 1960's in many dioceses.

But the need for these Catholic support groups no longer seems
necessary. As a result, Catholic organizations, service groups, and
schools are closing for lack of members and financial support--support
that at one time came so willingly from those who had far less to spare
than do present-day Catholics.

As a result these organizations are changing their emphases to
include a wider, and not necessarily Catholic, membership. For example,
the Catholic Sodalities have become Christian Life Communities and many
Catholic schools, especially in black communities, have a majority of
non-Catholic students.

This trend toward assimilation among Catholics explains, at least
in part, the discrepancy between the value orientations of the laity and
the official stance of the Catholic Church. American Catholics are in
the middle of American society and because of this, they are reflecting
the cultural values and religious membership patterns of their fellow
Americans to a greater extent than ever before.

As a result of this shift, we must now look to the American
situation as a whole to understand what is happening in the American
Catholic Church.

Cultural Reasons

We mentioned at the beginning of this chapter that the American Catholic Church is becoming a voluntary religion. We will look at this American phenomenon more closely.

The roots of American voluntarism, especially in the religious sphere, go back to the origins of the country itself. Sidney Ahlstrom writes about the appearance of voluntarism at the time of the American Revolution.

> Statesmen and denominational leaders solved the problems of American pluralism in the only way that was consonant with the ideals and necessities of the American Revolution. The form of church life that resulted from these revolutionary developments depended on the voluntary support of a committed laity. This typically American arrangement was accompanied by certain other developments, even in the Roman Catholic Church: a tendency to foster the democratically governed local church and to discount or oppose hierarchies and higher judicatories of the church, a concern for practical achievements rather than doctrinal purity, and a pervasive and growing disinclination for formalism in worship, intellectualism in theology, and other worldly conceptions of piety and morality. Because the religious situation became more competitive, ministers were obliged to please their constituencies--and hence lost authority and status. Naturally there were many who viewed the future of religion and the churches with foreboding (Ahlstrom, 1972:382).

This experience of competition for the voluntary membership of the laity has continued in the Protestant churches to the present. But in the Catholic Church the mass influx of Catholic immigrants pushed voluntarism into the background. All energies were spent on meeting the religious, social, and economic needs of these people.

But the pressing problems of cultural identity and assimilation into the culture for these ethnic groups have been met, and the experience of voluntarism has now returned to the Catholic Church. Since Catholics now identify with the dominant culture, they also share its stress on democratic government, the discounting of hierarchies, the emphasis on practical achievement, and the disinclination for formalism. They consider many aspects of the Church to be out of touch with the American culture and, at times, find it getting in the way of their participation in that culture.

This trend toward voluntarism also provides clues as to why the majority of the laity wish to keep the Church out of sociopolitical affairs. The American "way of life" has stressed the compartmentalization of religion into a sphere of activity all its own, independent of the sociopolitical sphere. This is one aspect of American voluntarism that is evident in today's Catholic population. Americans have been jealous of this Church-State dichotomy and Catholics now share this attitude. The strong individualistic, voluntaristic emphasis of American culture, which allows the person to make up his own mind, do his own thing, and go his own way, is as strong among Catholics as it is in the rest of the American population. This attitude is becoming apparent in the freedom which Catholics feel to attend Church when and where they like and to make up their own minds on personal and social moral matters. They feel, like their fellow Americans, that they have a choice in these moral and religious areas. The American Catholic Church, in other words, is becoming a voluntary religion.

There is another cultural influence that is affecting Church affiliation that, unlike voluntarism, is a recent arrival on the American scene. It is the "drop-out" phenomenon.

There is evidence that Americans are experiencing a growing dissatisfaction with the American culture. Because of its pragmatic past, the country has developed a highly efficient and specialized culture. Three characteristics have emerged: urbanization, with its stress on division of labor and impersonal, functional forms of interaction among people, bureaucratization, with its stress on efficiency, specific codes of behavior and detailed job-descriptions, and technology, with its stress on precision, speed, and expansion. These ingredients of our culture are held up as the keys to America's future and destiny. Today's Americans, however, are not so sure these characteristics of the American "way of life" still lead to a meaningful future.[2]

There were examples of this loss of faith in our survey of lay attitudes. For instance, only half of both Catholic and Protestant groups said they felt optimistic about America's future. Nor were they convinced that the American political or economic system was the best form of social organization. Table 5-1 gives their response.

In each case only a minority of the respondents, and in some cases only a small minority, were convinced that the American system was the best. Nor did the Catholic and Protestant groups differ appreciably in their responses, varying by no more than ten percentage points.

TABLE 5-1

CATHOLIC AND PROTESTANT CLERGY AND LAITY FAVORABLE
RESPONSE TO THE AMERICAN SYSTEM, BY PERCENT

	Catholic		Protestant	
The American System is Best[a]	Clergy	Laity	Clergy	Laity
1. Economic system	23	30	30	37
2. Political system	41	38	38	48

[a]The survey was taken in early 1972, before the Watergate controversy.

There seems to be, in other words, a growing discontent among many Americans with the American pragmatic (i.e., urban, bureaucratic, and technological) way of life. They feel powerless in the face of such a large, impersonal, and efficient system. These feelings of powerlessness by the individual are causing many Americans to react against the system. Direct confrontation seems to have had little impact, as was proven by the protests and confrontations of the 1960's. A less direct reaction is now being used by many people. It consists in withdrawing from, or "dropping-out" of, the dominant American culture.

This withdrawal takes many forms ranging from migration out of the country to simply not doing the job that a person is programmed to do. Job absenteeism is becoming a prominent worry in the business world and managers are trying every way they know of to motivate the American working force.[3]

The withdrawal is a complex phenomenon. It exists in many different segments of the population and for many different reasons.[4] One segment, for instance, consists of the recently-ethnic group who tend to be toward the conservative end of the socioeconomic spectrum. These individuals have only recently been integrated into the mainstream of society through hard work and sacrifice. Once there, they now see society taking their new status away from them by means of housing ordinances, integration laws, and leniency toward protest groups. Their reaction to this flux is an unconscious frustration that their new fought-for status is not recognized by the culture any more. The urban-bureaucratic leveling process has taken away any prestige they thought they would be enjoying once they escaped from their ethnic culture. The result is a love-hate relationship with society. On the love side, they want desperately to share the success and fortune of the American dream. But on the hate side, they are disgruntled because the dream is growing vague and uncertain. Their response is a subtle withdrawal from cooperating in or contributing to the American "way of life," a way of life which is now failing to protect their interests. Their withdrawal takes the form of apathy, lack of initiative, and an "I-don't-give-a-damn" form of absenteeism. One example of this pessimistic attitude was the much lower favorable response to the American economic and political systems among the parishioners belonging to the more ethnic-oriented parish. Only 28 percent of them thought that the American political system was the world's best, and 20 percent thought our economic system to be the best. These responses were both ten percentage points below the average Catholic lay response.

Another group of people that is having second thoughts about their place in the culture comes from the middle class. It consists of people who are the mainstays of the culture but are now becoming disenchanted with the system because of its control over individual creativity and initiative.

This group is on the other end of the spectrum from the first group since they have experienced the American dream of success long enough to know what it has to offer, and they are beginning to realize that it is not enough. The growing number of "drop-outs" from the middle class, especially among the young, express their disenchantment in various ways--drugs, protests, new life-styles, and leaving the country altogether. They see no future in contributing to the American culture as it now exists. But what does this have to do with the shifting patterns of membership in the American Catholic Church?

Since the Catholic Church is itself a large, bureaucratic and, in some of its aspects, an impersonal institution, people are unconsciously (perhaps a few consciously) rejecting this institution in the same manner as they reject other bureaucratic and impersonal institutions in American culture.[5] It is likely that they do this even before they "drop-out" of the other institutions since there are few reprisals for not attending Church. One does not get "fired" for religious withdrawal. One possible reason, then, for the drop in parish participation is that many Catholics are reacting to the Church in the same way as they react to the American society and are now, more than ever before, tempted to withdraw their support of the institutional Church.

This withdrawal seems to be coming from both ends of the traditional-progressive spectrum, i.e., from those who have only recently emerged from the religious, ethnic ghetto and from those who have been integrated from birth into the culture.

The traditional group is disturbed by the changing character of the Church since Vatican II, a Church they considered to be built on the rock of Peter and thus unchangeable. They feel powerless and unable to cope with the new doctrines coming from their parishes and schools and so register their discontent by withholding support of these institutions and activities. They do this by taking their children out of the schools, by hanging on to the traditional forms of devotion and worship, by not contributing to the building and expansion funds and finally, in exasperation, by giving up the Mass and sacraments altogether. Their Church no longer protects their interests or meets their needs. In a word, they have lost faith in the institutional Church.

On the other end of the spectrum lie the progressive Catholics. They were probably at one time highly involved in Catholic programs and have given years of service to the Church, possibly as a priest or religious. But due to the inconsistencies between the empirical structure and the spiritual ideal, they have grown at first angry, then frustrated, and finally apathetic. This is so because they discover that their own efforts are to no avail in attempting a solution. The institution is too cumbersome to be flexible. The result is withdrawal from the structure in pursuit of a more authentic expression of their religious ideals.

This is why the mainline Protestant churches are themselves experiencing a drop in parish involvement in proportions similar to the Catholic parishes.[6] It also explains why fundamentalist and revivalist religions are experiencing an increase in membership. These groups speak, however simplistically, to the needs of people who feel left out of the larger, more bureaucratic churches. This might also explain why Catholic Pentecostalism is drawing a large following, since it, too, speaks to a felt need in its stress on religious experience and group solidarity.[7]

This experience of powerlessness and frustration in the face of a large, hierarchical, and bureaucratic Church is one reason for the shift in parish membership. What is important to note, however, is that we are dealing, in many instances, with a cultural rather than a religious phenomenon. It is not the Church that may be at fault. It may be, instead, a crisis of American identity.

This is not to deny that many religious and "Church" related aspects are involved in the changing patterns of Church membership among the people. We will now look at a few of these theological and religious reasons for shifting membership patterns.

Theological Reasons

There can be little doubt that Catholics have been influenced by the changes that have been going on in the Church since Vatican II. They have had an impact on the people's association and identification with the institutional Church. The changes that have affected Catholics most have been in the areas of liturgical modes of worship, the meaning of "Church" and moral decision-making.

There has been a profound shift in liturgical practices among Catholics in the past ten years. The underlying motive has been to allow Catholics to become more involved in worship and in the Mass. What in 1960 was a highly ritualistic exercise of mystery performed in Latin by a priest whose back was turned to the people, by 1970 had become a participative act of communal worship, said in English and led (not performed) by a "principal celebrant" in union with all those celebrating with him.

The change was as sudden and complete as any tradition that had lasted for so many centuries could possibly be. In the wake of this change, not only did many of the old traditions and rituals connected with the celebration of the Mass go by the board, but so did the devotions, litanies, rosaries, novenas, and benedictions, i.e., all those rituals that in the "old days" filled the participative needs that the Mass did not provide.

Once the Mass changed to a communal, involving type of worship service, the other acts of worship and devotion received less emphasis. This all happened in the space of less than ten years.

It was inevitable that the people were left confused and bewildered by these sudden changes. Even the priests felt the strain. One of the tragedies during the period of adjustment following Vatican II was the lack of education and instruction, on all levels, as to the meaning and purpose of these liturgical changes. The people were not given the proper perspective or theological grounding that was necessary if the changes were to be accepted and understood.

This was especially true for the parish priests. They were no
better prepared than were their people for the sudden shift. As a result
many of them were themselves suspicious and confused with the changes,
and the parishioners could sense this. There was a sense of doubt among
the parishioners that the new liturgies would be an improvement over the
old or that their priests could lead them in the appreciation of the
innovations.

The difficulty over liturgical changes affected both young and
old. The older groups were familiar with the old liturgies and were
content to have the priest perform the liturgies. In the new rites the
people were required to join in the responses and the singing, instead
of leaving them up to the servers and the choir. It was no longer
possible to follow along at your own pace or say your rosary during Mass.

The young people, on the other hand, felt abandoned by the Church
because the priests had not understood the new ritual and were hesitant
to let the people contribute their own songs and prayers to the liturgy.
As a result, they, too, became disinterested in the parish liturgies because they did not speak their language or meet their needs. This disenchantment from young and old alike helps explain why there was a drop
in Mass attendance and parish involvement on all age levels.

The second area of change concerns changes in the meaning of
"Church." It was not many years ago when the Church, at least in the
minds of the people, considered itself the only true way to salvation.
Outside the Church there was no salvation. The Protestant churches were
unfortunate aberrations of the one, true Church and any contact with
Protestants was suspect.

But recently a new concept of the Church has filtered down to
the people. Ecumenical services are permitted and even encouraged.
Mixed marriages are performed in the church instead of in the rectory
--they may not even be in a Catholic Church! There have been statements
from Catholic theologians, and from Vatican II itself, that Protestant
religions can make a contribution to a fuller understanding of the
Catholic Church. The term "anonymous Christianity" has been used to explain how people who try to follow their conscience are implicit Christians although they may not know about or admit Christianity.

The Catholic laity have begun to realize that the one, holy,
catholic and apostolic Church is no longer an absolute. The boundaries
are no longer clear and distinct and it is hard to tell who is "in" and
who is "out."

John N. Kotre, in The View from the Border, conducted interviews with fifty graduate students who said they were Catholics and with fifty who said they once were but no longer considered themselves such. He found it difficult to separate the two groups by external religious practices or value orientations. His conclusion states:

> The borderline remains blurred in the sense that there is no universally accepted definition of what it takes to be Catholic. Thus it is still possible to find self-defined Catholics less overtly Catholic than others who have left the Church (Kotre, 1971:176).

There is operating in Catholicism, then, a widening concept of Church which allows for a greater degree of diversity and pluralism. The effects this has on parish involvement are varied. Some of the traditional, and in some cases, less educated parishioners have become frustrated by this liberal understanding of Church and have the feeling that the Church is collapsing around them. They become angry, confused, and alienated. The result is withdrawal from parish activities.

Others, especially the more theologically educated, are taking advantage of the widening concept of Church and are expressing their identification with the Catholic Church in ways other than attending the local parish. They feel free to find faith groups that better meet their needs and share their religious attitudes than does their parish or their clergy.

For others, this relative definition of Church means an apathetic withdrawal of Church support. The guilt feelings and fear of committing a mortal sin no longer are strong enough to assure Mass attendance or parish involvement. This last attitude brings up the question of moral decision-making, the third area of change.

There has been a shift in Catholic moral theology from a dogmatic, do-as-we-say-we-know-best attitude to a "fundamental option" approach. The first attitude held that all human beings were free but they needed help to know what was a mortal sin and what was not. Sexual mores, abstinence laws, Mass obligations--these were all spelled out in detail so that there could be little doubt when you were in sin and when you were not.

But lately there has been a shift in emphasis. The fast from midnight before receiving Holy Communion was reduced, the Friday abstinence from eating meat was dropped, the Sunday obligation of Mass attendance was shifted to include Saturday evening as well. One could even marry a Protestant and have a full Catholic wedding. All these things were now permitted and a person could still be a Catholic of high standing in doing them.

The laity began to wonder just where the line was to be drawn. When they asked an authority (priest, sister, religious teacher), they were told that what mattered was a person's intention or motivation and how this related to his "fundamental option."

What they meant was that individual choices and decisions in a person's life are ratifications and articulations of a basic orientation for good or evil, that is, opting for oneself and one's own pleasure before anything else or opting for love and concern for the needs of others. All other choices are to be judged in light of this fundamental option.

What has happened in this new emphasis on intentionality and motivation is to shift the importance of individual moral choices from being objective and absolute in themselves to placing them within the context of the person's intention in making the choices.

This change in emphasis from objective to subjective morality has had great ramifications on Catholic practices and attitudes over the last ten years. The individual Catholic is not sure why but he is aware that many of the absolutes the Church once held sacred are no longer "on the books." It is now up to the individual Catholic to make the choice, with, of course, the help and direction of the Church.[8] It is _his_ choice, _he_ is the one who must ultimately decide. The result is that the people's choices in personal and social moral value areas do not always coincide with the official position of the Catholic Church. They feel that _they_ are the ones who must decide and _they_ are the ones who are responsible for their choices.

These, then, are three areas of changes within the Catholic Church that have taken place in recent years and are influencing the people's patterns of Church identification and association with the parish.

Conclusion

We have tried to point out various reasons why there is a shift in parish membership patterns taking place in the American Catholic Church today. We are dealing with a complicated phenomenon and we cannot hope to provide all the reasons for the current situation. We have dealt with only a few.

First, there is the historical shift from an identification with a self-conscious, apologetic Church to an identification with a pluralistic, American culture. Being a member of the Catholic Church no longer separates people from this culture.

We have also looked at some of the cultural influences on Church membership, the growing disenchantment with bureaucratic institutions in any form and the participation of the Catholic population in the democratic, voluntaristic character of American religions.

And, finally, we have considered a few of the internal, theological reasons for shifting membership patterns that have become apparent since the Second Vatican Council in the areas of worship, the understanding of Church, and moral decision-making.

The dominant theme that seems to run through all these explanations is the spreading out of the membership in the Catholic Church. What was once easily identified by Mass attendance, reception of the sacraments, and allegiance to a code of moral conduct, is now an amorphous group of people who profess belief in a single religion, but whose beliefs and practices manifest a great diversity and plurality of forms.

We have now come to the end of our study of shifting membership in a changing Church. We have tried to catch the tempo of the present-day Church in a period of transition and have suggested reasons why this transition and change are taking place at this time. There have been limitations to all these areas of discussion. We are only touching the surface of a rich and complex reality, the American Catholic Church. The worth of such discussion and study is its relationship to the larger perspective of the Church's ultimate meaning and purpose. If it helps uncover and give understanding to how this meaning is being reflected in the lives and attitudes of the present-day Catholic, then it has been a worthwhile endeavor.

NOTES

CHAPTER I

1. See in particular Andrew Greeley and William C. McCready, (1973:1) and George Gallup, (1974).

2. The study was conducted under the auspices of the Center for the Scientific Study of Religion located in Chicago. The study was under the direction of Dr. W. Widick Schroeder, Assistant Secretary and Assistant Treasurer of the Center. A full report of the study is available under the title Suburban Religion (see Reference Section).

3. Because the study did not have the resources to canvas the area in order to uncover all the Catholics who were not declared members of the parish, a valuable segment of the Catholic population was lost. Joseph Fichter, S.J., (1954:73) discovered twenty years ago, in an era when the parish structure was a more stable and all-inclusive unity than it is today, that approximately one-third of those baptized in the Church were non-practicing or non-declared Catholics and could not be considered as members of the parish.

CHAPTER II

1. The higher percentage in favor of change among the Catholic clergy may be an indication of greater ferment in the Catholic Church rather than a resistance to change among the Protestant and Jewish clergy. These latter come from traditions that have had to adapt to cultural and religious changes over a long period of time and, therefore, their desire for further change is not a pressing problem for them.

2. A good example of pre-Vatican II parish life can be found in Joseph Fichter, S.J.'s excellent studies, (1951 and 1954).

3. Since only five of the seventy-nine non-Catholic clergy in the sample were Jewish (6 percent), the differences between the Catholic and other clergy groups were largely due to the Protestant responses.

4. It is interesting to note that the fundamentalists among the Protestant clergy are even less favorable toward recreational activities in the parish (30 percent). This is in keeping with their skeptical attitude toward "worldly" behavior.

5.   Only 30 percent of the clergy serving fundamentalist congregations were favorable toward such activities. This, again, is an indication of the dichotomy they find between the "worldly" and the "godly."

6.   This seems to be in disagreement with the national survey of priests in which "only one-fifth think the Church would be helped by closing of the parochial schools." (Greeley, 1972b:147). This discrepancy might be explained by the difference in the wording of the question. In the national survey the priests were asked whether they thought the Church would be helped by the elimination of the Catholic school system. In the survey under study here the question was much simpler and closer to home. The clergy were asked, "What is your attitude toward your present parish school?" See also the evaluation of the Greeley study (Hughes, et al. 1973:7,9) for a critique of the wording and analysis of the parochial school question in the national survey.

7.   For a discussion of the changing attitudes toward Catholic schools, see Andrew M. Greeley, (1973) especially Chapter VIII, "From Parochial Schools to Human Development."

8.   Andrew Greeley, (1972b:253) states: "At the time the data in this report were collected, about 3 percent of the priests in the sample were definitely or probably going to leave the priesthood in the near future. About 22 percent of the priests, thirty-five and under, were either going to leave or were at least uncertain about their future in the ministry. A large proportion of American priests have rethought their own position because of the departure of friends from the priest-hood."

9.   See also the critique of this comparison in the evaluation of the Greeley report (Hughes, et al. 1973:26).

10. If, however, we were to separate the mainline Protestant clergy response from the fundamentalist groups, we would find a closer resemblance between the Catholic clergy response on this issue (63 per-cent) and the responses of clergy (67 percent) serving more established Protestant congregations.

11. See Greeley, (1972b:187-191) for reading habits of priests in the national survey. The results published there showed greater interest in theological reading and up-dating than our survey uncovered. Perhaps the difference is the specialized character of the priests in this study, all of them serving large suburban parishes. The Greeley survey sampled a wider spectrum of clergy including religious priests and those in specialized ministries.

12. The Catholic Pentecostal movement is now being studied and reports from these studies should be available soon. In personal correspondence received from Reverend Joseph Fichter, S.J., he stated, "There are at least a half-dozen sociologists around the country now doing research on Catholic Pentecostalism. By this time next year there ought to be a flood of information about the movement." The letter was dated 18 June, 1973.

13. If we were to compare only those Protestant clergy serving churches affiliated with the National Council of Churches, i.e., the more established churches, the difference is even more striking, 81 percent versus 18 percent!

14. "There is also no longer majority support for the official teaching on divorce. Only 40 percent of the active diocesan priests and 43 percent of the active religious priests are willing to exclude all possibility of divorce." (Greeley, 1972b:115).

15. This discrepancy may be due to the suburban pastoral character of the priests involved in this sample.

16. The national survey of the priesthood reports the resignation rate from the priesthood was about 5 percent between the years 1966 to 1969 (Greeley, 1972b:259, 313).

CHAPTER III

1. This is not the case for Protestant membership in which the person who wishes to belong to a particular church must formally declare himself a member.

2. George Gallup found that 42 percent of the Catholics polled did not consider it a sin to miss Mass on Sunday even when one could have easily attended (Gallup, 1971:Table 11).

3. See Appendix B, for a discussion of the survey of Catholic students' religious attitudes and practices.

4. See Appendix A, for the construction of this measure of parish involvement.

5. Joseph Fichter, S.J., (1954:17, 22) constructed these categories in his study of parish life. He labeled the last category, however, dormant instead of nominal members as we have done.

6.   See the Appendix for the construction of this and other indices used in this chapter.

7.   See Chapter II, Table 2-13, p. 32.   Similar declines were reported by Greeley and McCready in an unpublished study of religious practices.   See National Catholic Reporter, X (November 16, 1973).

CHAPTER IV

1.   The contraception issue is not included because the position of the Church on this question, at least at the parish level, is not clear, and it is difficult to base a conclusion as to how well Catholics internalize the Catholic Church's moral teachings on this issue.   See Greeley, (1972b:111): "In every age group of the priests, confessional practice on the subject of birth control has grown more 'liberal' since the issuance of Humanae Vitae."   See also McCormick, (1970:30-33).

2.   See "On Race Relations and Poverty," Pastoral Statement of the National Catholic Conference of Bishops, November 18, 1966, and more recently "Poverty Profile" of the Campaign for Human Development, NCCB, 1972.

3.   The people were, in fact, more open to a married clergy than were the clergy themselves.   Only 41 percent of the clergy were in favor of a married priesthood and another 23 percent had mixed feelings.

CHAPTER V

1.   There has been a recent revival of interest in ethnic identity (See Novak, 1971, Greeley, 1971, and Abramson, 1973)   It is our contention, however, that the pluralism that is becoming more and more noticeable in the Catholic Church runs along common interest and value lines rather than along national or ethnic lines.   In other words, the diversity of the American Church, while not discounting the influence of its ethnic past, is more a difference of expectations or even ideology than of cultural orig

2.   See Ahlstrom, (1972:1087) in which he describes various senti- ments of the 1960's to include "a creeping (or galloping) awareness of vast contradictions in American life between profession and performance, the ideal and the actual."

3.   One example is "The Job Blahs: Who Wants to Work?", which was the cover story in the March 26, 1973 issue of Newsweek.

4.   Ahlstrom, (1972:1094) remarks in his chapter on "The Turbulent Sixties," "Americans, whether conservative, liberal or radical, found it increasingly difficult to believe that the United States was still a beacon to the world."

5.   Sidney Ahlstrom makes this connection in his discussion of religion in the 1960's: "The declining growth rates and widespread budgetary problems of all the large denominations clearly reveals a loss of institutional vitality--though this loss was also experienced by every other institution as well" (1972:1086).

6.   There was a 31 percent drop in parish involvement among the Protestant laity compared with a 28 percent drop among the Catholics in the survey reported in previous chapters.

7.   Ahlstrom also noted this turn to fundamentalism in a foot-note to his discussion of the 1960's: "Equally relevant was the many-faceted evangelical revival that manifested itself in the late 1960's. Appearing first was a charismatic revival that soon flowed beyond the Pentecostal churches into staid middle-class denominations and the student population. By 1971 there were even ten thousand or more Roman Catholic Pentecostals with both clergy and nuns among them" (1972:1086 n).

8.   This helps explain why the clergy in our survey were more willing to give direction than provide the answers to the people's problems. See Chapter II, p. 26.

APPENDIX

1.   See Kotre, (1971:Chapter VII) for a discussion of male versus female membership in religious groups.

2.   See Gallup, (1971), Greeley, (1972b) and Greeley and McCready, (1973).

<u>REFERENCES</u>

Abramson, Harold
    1973 <u>Ethnic Diversity in Catholic America</u>. New York: John Wiley
          and Sons.
Ahlstrom, Sidney E.
    1972 <u>A Religious History of the American People</u>. New Haven,
          Connecticut: Yale University Press.
Cogley, John
    1973 <u>Catholic America</u>. New York: Dial Press.
Fichter, Joseph
    1968 <u>America's Forgotten Priests--What They are Saying</u>. New York:
          Harper and Row.
    1954 <u>Social Relations in the Urban Parish</u>. Chicago: University
          of Chicago Press.
    1951 <u>Dynamics of a City Church</u>. Chicago: University of Chicago
          Press.
    1965 <u>Priest and People</u>. New York: Sheed and Ward.
Gallup, George
    1971 <u>Religion in America</u>. Princeton, New Jersey: Gallup
          International.
    1974 "Churchgoing Decline of Last Decade, Result of Sliding
          Catholic Attendance." Chicago: Hall Syndicate. Jan. 13, 19
Gannon, S.J., Thomas M.
    1972 The Internal Social Organization of Belief Systems of
          American Priests. Unpublished Ph.D. dissertation, University
          of Chicago.
Gleason, Philip (ed.)
    1969 <u>Contemporary Catholicism in the U.S.</u> Notre Dame, Indiana:
          University of Notre Dame Press.
    1970 <u>Catholicism in America</u>. New York: Harper and Row.
Greeley, Andrew M.
    1973 <u>The New Agenda</u>. Garden City, New York: Doubleday and
          Company, Inc.
    1972a <u>Priests in the United States, Reflections on a Survey</u>.
          Garden City, New York: Doubleday and Company, Inc.
    1972b <u>The Catholic Priest, Sociological Investigations</u>. Washington,
          D.C.: U.S. Catholic Conference Press.
    1971 <u>Why Can't They be Like Us? America's White Ethnic Groups</u>.
          New York: E. P. Dutton.
Greeley, Andrew M. and William C. McCready
    1973 "Drop in Churchgoing 'Catastrophic'" <u>National Catholic</u>
          <u>Reporter</u>. Nov. 16, 1973.
Herberg, Will
    1955 <u>Protestant, Catholic, Jew</u>. Garden City, New York: Anchor
          Books.

Houtart, Francois
    1968   The Eleventh Hour, Exposition of a Church. New York:
            Sheed and Ward.
Hughes, Everett C., Salley Whelan Cassidy and John D. Donovan
    1973   An Evaluation of the Catholic Priest in the United States
            Sociological Investigations. Washington, D.C.: U.S.
            Catholic Conference Press.
Kennedy, Eugene C. and Victor J. Heckler
    1971   The Catholic Priest in the United States, Psychological
            Investigations. Washington, D.C.: U.S. Catholic Conference
            Press.
Kotre, John
    1971   A View from the Border. Chicago: Aldine-Atherton.
Larkin, O. Carm., Ernest E. and Gerald T. Broccolo
    1973   Spiritual Renewal of American Priesthood. Washington, D.C.:
            U.S. Catholic Conference Press.
Lenski, Gerhard
    1961   The Religious Factor. Garden City, New York: Doubleday
            and Company, Inc.
McCormick, Richard A.
    1973   "The Silence Since 'Humanae Vitae'." America, CXXIX
            (July 21, 1973), 30-33.
National Conference of Catholic Bishops
    1966   Pastoral Statement on Race Relations and Poverty. Washington,
            D.C.: U.S. Catholic Conference Press.
    1972   Poverty Profile, for the Campaign for Human Development.
            Washington, D.C.: U.S. Catholic Conference Press.
Novak, Michael
    1971   The Rise of the Unmeltable Ethnics. New York: MacMillan
            Company
O'Brien, David J.
    1972   The Renewal of American Catholicism. New York: Oxford
            University Press.
O'Connor, John (ed.)
    1968   The American Catholic Exodus. Washington, D.C.: Corpus
            Press.
O'Dea, Thomas
    1969   Alienation, Atheism, and the Religious Crisis. New York:
            Sheed and Ward.
Robertson, D. B. (ed.)
    1966   Voluntary Associations. Richmond, Virginia: John Knox
            Press.
Schroeder, W. Widick, Victor Obenhaus, Larry A. Jones and Thomas Sweetser, S.J.
    1974   Suburban Religion. Chicago: Center for the Scientific Study
            of Religion.

Smith, Constance and Anne Freedman
    1972   Voluntary Associations.   Cambridge, Massachusetts:
        Harvard University Press.
Smith, Elwyn A.
    1970   The Religion of the Republic.   Philadelphia: Fortress
        Press.
United States Department of Commerce, Bureau of the Census
    1971   1970 Census of Population, Number of Inhabitants.   PC(1)-A1.
    1972   1970 Census of Population, General Population Characteristics.
        PC(1)-B1.
Wills, Garry
    1972   Bare Ruined Choirs.   New York: Doubleday and Company, Inc.

APPENDICES

APPENDIX A

CONSTRUCTION OF INDICES

A number of indices were constructed and used in the analyses reported in Chapters III and IV. They have been discussed in various passages, but they have not always been elaborated. This appendix shows how these indices were constructed from the questionnaire responses. They are arranged in the order in which they appear in the text.

1. Index of Parish Membership.

This index was constructed by combining the responses to the question of Mass attendance and the level of participation in parish activities. Those who went to Mass regularly and took part in at least two other parish functions or activities were termed "nuclear" members. Those who fulfilled their Mass attendance obligation but were not involved in at least two other parish functions or activities were termed "modal" members. Those who attended Mass once a month or so were termed "marginal," and those who attended Mass on rare occasions were termed "nominal" members.

2. Index of Parish Participation Trends.

This index served as a measure of change in parish involvement over the last five years. It summarized the responses to the questions concerning a person's level of Mass attendance now compared with five years ago, involvement in parish activities now versus five years ago, and size of contributions to the parish now versus five years ago. The index was weighted so that the question on contribution levels had only half the weight of the other two questions since it was not considered as strong a measure of parish participation as Mass attendance or participation in parish activities. The index was divided into these four categories: those who were shifting toward greater involvement now than in the past, those whose parish participation had remained unchanged, those who were at present shifting toward less parish participation and those whose parish participation had dropped drastically in the last five years.

3. Index of Liturgical Attitudes.

There have been many changes in liturgical forms in parishes since Vatican II, and this index was constructed to learn how Catholics react to these changes and whether they favored progressive or traditional forms of worship services. The index was constructed from the compound question concerning reactions to a list of various liturgical practices.

The list used for the index included: Guitar Mass with contemporary hymns, Informal Masses in homes, the "Kiss-of-Peace" in Mass, Laymen receiving Communion in the hand, Baptism during Mass and Laymen distributing Holy Communion. These responses were scored as follows:

> 1 = very favorable
> 2 = favorable
> 3 = mixed feelings
> 4 = unfavorable
> 5 = very unfavorable

Two other types of liturgical functions were also included, Quiet Masses with no responses, and Benediction and Evening Devotions, but these were scored in reverse order:

> 1 = very unfavorable
> 2 = unfavorable
> 3 = mixed feelings
> 4 = favorable
> 5 = very favorable

The total scores from these nine items were grouped into three categories:

> Progressive   Score: (8-20)
> Status Quo   (21-34)
> Traditional   (35-45)

4. Index of Personal Moral Values.

This index was based on the responses to four questions: "It is wrong for people to have pre-marital sexual relations," "It is wrong for married people to have sexual relations with persons other than their husbands or wives," "Divorce is wrong," and "It is wrong for a woman who wants an abortion in the first three months of pregnancy to have one." Responses to each question were assigned the following scores:

Strongly agree and Agree = 1
Mixed feelings and Depends on Circumstances = 2
and Disagree and Strongly Disagree = 3

The scores were summed and the following groupings for the index were made:

Orthodox Moral Stance	Score:	(4-6)
Circumstantial Stance		(7-9)
Lenient Moral Stance		(10-12)

5. Index of Parish Public Policy Involvement.

This index was constructed by summarizing the response to the item on the way the local parish should involve itself in social issues. The index was divided into four levels of parish involvement; High, Medium, Low, and None. The high response included those who felt the parish should either take official stands on public issues or help establish informal parish social action groups, or both. The medium response included those who thought the parish should form discussion groups in the parish to discuss public issues, or allow church facilities to be used by social action groups, or both. This group would not go so far, however, as to allow the parish to form informal action groups or take an official stand on public issues. The low response included those who would only agree to the parish giving help to people to join community social action groups not identified with the parish. The none response included those who felt the parish should not become involved in public policy in any form.

APPENDIX B

NON-RESPONDENTS

An attempt was made both through a telephone contact (and personal contact in Satellite City) and in consultation with the parish staffs to discover something about the non-respondents to see if they represented a group not found in the attitudes and feelings of those who had responded to the questionnaire.

The telephone interview included seven items from the questionnaire: age, sex, educational background, frequency of Mass attendance, attitudes toward the local parish, how they felt about recent changes in the Church and how they reacted to the Church taking a public stand on political issues. Tables A-1 through A-7 show the comparison of the questionnaire respondents and those interviewed by phone.

In general, the high percentage of return and the information contained in the responses indicates that sufficient data were received from all categories of age, sex, Church-affiliation and ethnic, economic, and educational backgrounds to make a representative analysis of the data possible. There were, however, some categories that were under-represented and these deserve comment.

1. Age Distribution. Since the sample was taken from the parish lists, and since these lists were made up of family entries rather than of individual members, the names of those twenty-five years old and younger were not always available. This was so either because they were away at school or because they did not receive envelopes for contributing purposes or because their ages were not given and it was therefore impossible to tell whether they were old enough to receive a questionnaire.

As Table A-1 indicates, even for those included in the random sample, a lower percentage of the "Under 25" category returned the completed questionnaire than those who responded by telephone. This underrepresentation of young adults was the reason for adding supplementary material from another survey reported in the next section of this appendix.

Although Table A-1 does not show it, a greater percentage of those who refused to respond to the survey were elderly people. It appears from their comments over the telephone that they did not feel well enough or interested enough to respond. There were enough who did respond, however, to provide a balanced age distribution on the older end of the age spectrum.

TABLE A-1

AGE DISTRIBUTION

Age	Questionnaire Respondents		Telephone Respondents	
	No.	Pct.	No.	Pct.
Under 25	23	4	6	8
25-34	130	24	17	23
35-54	288	53	39	53
55 and Over	107	19	12	16
Total	548	100	74	100

TABLE A-2

SEX DISTRIBUTION

Sex	Questionnaire Respondents		Telephone Respondents	
	No.	Pct.	No.	Pct.
Men	210	39	34	47
Women	332	61	39	53
Total	542	100	73	100

2. Sex Distribution. Table A-2 indicates a greater response from women than from men. This was so for many reasons. First, the parish rolls themselves had a greater percentage of women members. There

were many widows, Catholic wives of mixed marriages, and wives separated
from their husbands which caused an over-balance of women members.[1]
Secondly, even though the directions on the questionnaire explicitly
stated that the person to whom it was sent was to fill it out, in many
cases the wife filled out the questionnaire for her husband, if he was
too busy or did not want to do it himself. Thirdly, even in the cases
where the wife did not fill out the questionnaire for her husband, it
often happened that the husband who did not complete the questionnaire
did respond to the telephone interview. For this reason there was a
higher percentage of men responding to the telephone interview than to
the questionnaire, as indicated in Table A-2. Controlling for the male-
female response, however, did not uncover any significant difference in
their responses to key questions and therefore the over-representation
of female respondents was not considered a drawback to the results of
the survey.

TABLE A-3

EDUCATIONAL LEVELS DISTRIBUTION

Highest Year of School Completed	Questionnaire Respondents		Telephone Respondents	
	No.	Pct.	No.	Pct.
Non-high school graduate	84	15	10	13
High school graduate	146	27	27	37
Some college	153	28	21	28
College graduate	85	16	8	11
Graduate school	68	14	8	11
Total	536	100	74	100

3. _Educational Distribution_. It became apparent from the higher
refusal rate in the lower status parish of Satellite City, and from the
comparison of questionnaire and telephone responses in Table A-3, that

those with a high school education or less did not respond to the survey
in equal numbers as did those with a college education or better. This
is to be expected since the lesser-educated groups are not as familiar
with survey instruments or filling out forms as are the professional or
college-educated group. There was the added problem that many of those
in the lower status area did not have telephones and therefore the followup procedures were more difficult and less effective. Despite these
drawbacks, the questionnaire sample did include a 42 percent response
from those with no more than a high school education which was judged
sufficient to represent the point of view of the non-college educated
and predominately blue-collar population.

TABLE A-4

FREQUENCY OF MASS ATTENDANCE DISTRIBUTION

Frequency of Attendance	Questionnaire Respondents		Telephone Respondents	
	No.	Pct.	No.	Pct.
Almost every week or more	401	72	45	61
Two or three times a month	36	7	7	10
Once a month	34	6	9	12
Two or three times a year	33	6	7	10
Never or almost never	48	9	6	8
Total	552	100	74	101

4. The Non-Active Parishioner. Table A-4 indicates that those
who did not attend Mass regularly were less likely to return the questionnaire than those who did. There is a reason for this. Those who
attend church regularly are those who are more closely identified with
the parish and are, therefore, more likely to take the time to fill out
a questionnaire related to something that they are associated with. Despite the under-representation of the marginal and nominal Catholics,

there were enough of those who did return the questionnaire (21 percent)
to allow for a comparison of their values and attitudes with those who
were more closely affiliated with the parish.

TABLE A-5

ATTITUDES TOWARD THE LOCAL PARISH DISTRIBUTION

Attitudes	Questionnaire Respondents		Telephone Respondents	
	No.	Pct.	No.	Pct.
Favorable	316	58	51	69
Mixed feelings	149	28	14	19
Unfavorable	42	8	8	11
No opinion	32	6	1	1
Total	539	100	74	100

5. Attitudinal Responses. There were three attitudinal questions included in the telephone interview which served as a comparison
with the questionnaire respondents. (See Table A-5 and Table A-7.) The
comparison of these responses shows first, that in the attitudes toward
the local parish, the telephone respondents expressed a more positive
position than did the questionnaire respondents. This is surprising,
especially considering that the telephone respondents contained a higher
percentage of those who do not attend the parish liturgies. One possible
explanation for the unexpected result is that when people are confronted
directly, even over the telephone, they are less likely to express negative
feelings toward the parish than they are when they respond by means of an
anonymous questionnaire. This might also explain the difference in the
questionnaire and telephone response to the role of the Church in the
political realm (see Table A-9). Once again, it was surprising to see
so many more of the telephone respondents agreeing with the statement
that the Church should take public stands on political issues. Table A-6
shows that the telephone respondents are not a more progressive group,
at least in relation to changes in the Church. It would seem, then, that

TABLE A-6

REACTION TO CHANGES IN THE CHURCH DISTRIBUTION

Attitudes Toward Changes	Questionnaire Respondents		Telephone Respondents	
	No.	Pct.	No.	Pct.
Desire slower rate of change	131	25	21	30
Are satisfied with present	186	35	32	46
Desire a faster rate of change	95	18	10	14
Are confused by the changes	91	17	5	7
No opinion	18	4	2	3
Total	521	99	70	100

TABLE A-7

REACTION TO THE CHURCH TAKING A STAND ON POLITICAL ISSUES

Attitudes	Questionnaire Respondents		Telephone Respondents	
	No.	Pct.	No.	Pct.
Agreement	71	13	22	31
Mixed feelings	109	20	17	24
Disagreement	333	61	29	41
No opinion	31	6	3	4
Total	544	100	71	100

the high response toward political involvement of the Church among the telephone respondents was due to the opportunity they had to qualify their responses. For example, a number of the respondents mentioned that they were in favor of the Church taking a stand on the political issues of abortion or aid to private schools but were not in favor of stands taken in connection with the war in Vietnam or integration.

These, then are the areas in which the representativeness of the sample had its limits. And yet, despite these limitations, it was still considered a valid sample of Catholic practice and opinion and a worth-while contribution to the growing volume of information on Catholic attitudes and feelings in the 1970's. That the findings reported here have found support in other studies is one indication of their validity and worth.[2]

Auxiliary Study of Catholic College Students

In order to make up for the under-representation of the "Under twenty-five" age category, additional data were borrowed from a study of Catholic college students' opinions undertaken by the author at Marquette University in Milwaukee and Loyola University in Chicago.

A random sample of undergraduate students was selected by choos-ing sections of philosophy and theology courses that all students were required to attend. A questionnaire was distributed to 400 students in each school in October of 1970 and again to another 400 students in each school in November of 1971. The purpose of the study was to discover what change, if any, had occurred between the two dates in the attitudes and religious practices of the students, and what influence, if any, the campus ministries programs in each school had on the attitudes and prac-tices of the students. The overall response rate for the two years was 75 percent.

The materials from that study that were used in this volume came from the responses to these questions:

49. While growing up I attended religious services. (Circle One)

1. Regularly   2. Occasionally   3. Hardly Ever   4. Never

50. I now attend religious services. (Circle One)

1. Regularly   2. Occasionally   3. Hardly Ever   4. Never

51. While growing up my religious affiliation was

_____

52. My religious affiliation at the present time is

_____

Table A-8 and Table A-9 summarizes the responses to these questions.

TABLE A-8

RELIGIOUS AFFILIATION OF CATHOLIC COLLEGE STUDENTS
(N=1192)

Religious Affiliation	Growing Up Percent	At Present Percent
1. Catholic	89	78
2. Protestant	3	2
3. Other	4	4
4. None	4	16
Total	100	100

TABLE A-9

CHURCH ATTENDANCE OF CATHOLIC COLLEGE STUDENTS
(N=1192)

Church Attendance	Growing Up Percent	At Present Percent
1. Regularly	93	52
2. Occasionally	5	21
3. Hardly ever	1	18
4. Never	1	9
Total	100	100

APPENDIX C

The Questionnaire

The questionnaire used with Catholic lay people is reproduced in
this appendix. Comparable questionnaires were employed with Protestant
and Jewish lay people. In these instances, the items on the Mass were
deleted and some minor changes in wording were made to fit the different
traditions. In the interests of economy, those schedules and the clergy
schedules, which were very comparable to the lay schedules, have not been
reproduced here.

LAY QUESTIONNAIRE

Please check the proper line, circle the proper number, or fill in the
proper blank. Feel free to write comments in the margin if you want.

I. Religious activities and attitudes

1. What is your present religious membership?

_____1) Catholic from birth   _____4) Jewish
_____2) Protestant   _____5) None
_____3) Catholic Convert (Please _____6) Other (please
         specify previous religion.)   specify)

_____   _____

1a. Name of church or local parish to which you belong: _____
_____

2. What is the present religious membership of your spouse?

_____1) Catholic from birth   _____4) Jewish
_____2) Protestant   _____5) None
_____3) Catholic Convert (Please _____6) I am not married.
         specify previous religion.) _____7) Other (please specify

_____   _____

3. Approximately how often do you attend Mass?

_____1) Almost every week or more   _____4) About two or three
_____2) About two or three times a   times a year
         month   _____5) Almost never
_____3) About once a month

113

4. Compared with five years ago, how often do you attend Mass now?

____1) Much more often now   ____4) Less often now
____2) More often now   ____5) Much less often now
____3) About the same

5. Compared with five years ago, how much money do you contribute to your parish now (excluding school tuition)?

____1) Much more now   ____4) Less now
____2) More now   ____5) Much less now
____3) About the same

6. Compared with five years ago, how much time do you spend in parish activities, programs and projects now?

____1) Much more time now   ____4) Less time now
____2) More time now   ____5) Much less time now
____3) About the same

7. A number of parishes have activities such as those specified below. Please indicate your feelings about such activities, whether your parish has them or not. For each activity circle the number under the heading which best expresses your feelings.

	Very Favorable	Favorable	Mixed Feelings	Unfavorable	Very Unfavorable	Don't Know Or No Opinion
1) Fund raising groups (Bake sales, bazaars, paper sales, etc.)	1	2	3	4	5	6
2) Experimental personal growth groups (Marathons, encounter groups, sensitivity groups, etc.)	1	2	3	4	5	6
3) Prayer and devotional groups (Pentecostal meetings, prayer meetings, etc.)	1	2	3	4	5	6
4) Recreational and social groups (Sports, potluck dinners, etc.)	1	2	3	4	5	6
5) Adult religious educational groups (Scripture study, adult discussion, etc.)	1	2	3	4	5	6
6) Service groups (Holy Name Society, women's club, etc.)	1	2	3	4	5	6

7) Social action groups (Community education, peace groups, civil rights groups, etc.)	1	2	3	4	5	6
8) Liturgy (Choir, Commentators, etc.)	1	2	3	4	5	6
9) Youth groups (CCD, Teen Club, etc.,--not including parish school)	1	2	3	4	5	6
0) Administrative and policy making groups (Parish Council, School Board, etc.)	1	2	3	4	5	6
1) Other groups (Please specify)	1	2	3	4	5	6

8. Are you a member of any groups or do you participate in any activities in your church? 1) Yes____   2) No____

8a. If yes, please list the group(s) or activity(ies).

Name of Group or Activity

_____

_____

_____

9. Have you ever taught CCD (Confraternity of Christian Doctrine) or been an advisor or teacher to a parish youth group? 1) Yes____   2) No____

    9a. If yes, what ages?

        ____1) Pre-school   ____4) Grades 10-12
        ____2) Grades 1-6   ____5) Adult
        ____3) Grades 7-9
    9b. If yes, for how many years altogether? ____years

10. About how far do you live from your church? ____miles

11. Do you frequently go to another church? 1) Yes____   2) No____

    11a. If yes, why? _____
    _____

12. Did you attend any church-related retreats, workshops, etc. in the last year? 1) Yes____   2) No____

12a. If yes, approximately how many? _____

13. Did you attend any church-related personal growth groups, such as
    sensitivity groups, encounter groups or marathons in the last year?

    1) Yes____   2) No____

    13a. If yes, approximately how many? ____

14. Have you had religious devotions or observances (such as prayers at
    meals or at night, Bible reading, etc.) in your home?

    1) Yes____   2) No____

    14a. If yes, check as many of the following as apply.

        ____1) Within the last year, special seasonal devotions at
                Advent, Christmas, Lent or Easter
        ____2) Within this past week, prayers at meals
        ____3) Within this past week, prayers at other times
        ____4) Within this past month, Bible reading
        ____5) Within this past month, other religious reading
        ____6) Within this last year, Masses in your home
        ____7) Other (please specify) _____

15. Approximately how often does your family or those with whom you live
    discuss the meaning of your faith for your daily lives?

    ____1) Almost every day   ____4) Only on special occasions
    ____2) About every week   ____5) Almost never
    ____3) About once or twice a month   ____6) I live alone.

16. During the past year, do you think your parish has engaged in any
    especially creative programs or activities?

    1) Yes____   2) No____   3) Don't Know____

    16a. If yes, please specify._____
    _____

17. What is your present attitude toward changes in the American Catholic
    Church? (Please check only one.)

    ____1) I was satisfied with the pre-Vatican II Church.
    ____2) I would like a slower rate of change.
    ____3) I am satisfied with the Church's present rate of change.
    ____4) I would like a more rapid rate of change in the future.
    ____5) I feel radical change is necessary in the Church.
    ____6) I am confused and uncertain about changes in the Church.
    ____7) I have no opinion one way or the other.

        Make any comments here:_____
    _____
    _____

18. What is your present general attitude toward the local parish?

____1) Very favorable   ____4) Unfavorable
____2) Favorable   ____5) Very unfavorable
____3) Mixed feelings   ____6) No opinion

Make any comments here:_____
_____
_____

18a. What is your present attitude toward the local parish school?

____1) Very favorable   ____4) Unfavorable
____2) Favorable   ____5) Very unfavorable
____3) Mixed feelings   ____6) No opinion

Make any comments here:_____
_____
_____

19. What is your feeling about the beliefs and practices of the following
religious groups? (Circle the number under the heading most closely
reflecting your attitude.)

	Very Favorable	Favorable	Mixed Feelings	Unfavorable	Very Unfavorable	Don't Know Or No Opinion
Catholic	1	2	3	4	5	6
Episcopalian	1	2	3	4	5	6
Lutheran	1	2	3	4	5	6
Jehovah's Witnesses	1	2	3	4	5	6
Judaism	1	2	3	4	5	6
Methodist	1	2	3	4	5	6
Presbyterian	1	2	3	4	5	6
Southern Baptist	1	2	3	4	5	6
United Church of Christ	1	2	3	4	5	6
Zen Buddhism	1	2	3	4	5	6

20. Excluding Catholics, which two religious groups listed in the preceding
question do you think have beliefs and practices most like the Catholic
Church?
1)_____   2)_____

Excluding Catholics, which two groups have beliefs and practices least
like the Catholic Church?
1)_____   2)_____

21. Consider for a moment the religious affiliation of your <u>four</u> closest friends.

    ____1) How many are Catholic?
    ____2) How many are Protestant?
    ____3) How many are Jewish?
    ____4) How many are not members of a church or synagogue?

22. Approximately what proportion of the relatives whom you see once a month or more are Catholic?

    ____1) All or almost all   ____4) About one-third
    ____2) About two-thirds   ____5) None or almost none
    ____3) About half   ____6) I don't see any relative once a month or more.

23. Listed below is a series of statements dealing with moral and religious matters. Indicate your reaction to each statement by circling the number under the heading which best expresses your feelings.

	Strongly Agree	Agree	Mixed Feelings	Disagree	Strongly Disagree	No Opinion
1) Priests today spend too much time talking about how people should behave and not enough about God and religious matters.	1	2	3	4	5	6
2) Being a Catholic makes it harder for me to feel I am part of American society.	1	2	3	4	5	6
3) Many Christians seem to think they are superior to other people.	1	2	3	4	5	6
4) There is no longer much difference between Catholic and Protestant churches.	1	2	3	4	5	6
5) The people I know who are faithful church members are less selfish than most other people I know.	1	2	3	4	5	6

6) Changes in the
    Mass make it
    harder for me to   1   2   3   4   5   6
    worship.

7) One should act as
    loving toward every-
    one as one does   1   2   3   4   5   6
    toward his family
    and close friends.

8) Catholic priests
    should be allowed
    to get married and   1   2   3   4   5   6
    still function
    as priests.

9) There are times when
    it might be all right
    to break one of the   1   2   3   4   5   6
    Ten Commandments.

10) Priests spend too
    much of their time
    condemning people   1   2   3   4   5   6
    for their sins.

11) We should make every
    effort to include
    all races and social   1   2   3   4   5   6
    classes in each
    local parish.

12) When I attend a good
    liturgy, I leave
    church resolved to
    try to improve my   1   2   3   4   5   6
    relations with my
    fellow men.

13) The Church should
    support Women's   1   2   3   4   5   6
    Liberation.

14) The Church should
    enforce a strict
    standard of moral   1   2   3   4   5   6
    conduct among its
    members.

15) The Church should
    be a place where one
    can go and find peace 1   2   3   4   5   6
    of mind and security.

16) The Church should take special note of major national holidays (Memorial Day and the Fourth of July).   1   2   3   4   5   6

17) The American Catholic Church should take public stands on political issues.   1   2   3   4   5   6

18) Jesus Christ is the necessary foundation for my religious faith.   1   2   3   4   5   6

19) We should seek to make all men Christians.   1   2   3   4   5   6

20) God changes as the world evolves.   1   2   3   4   5   6

23a. Indicate your feeling about the following types of parish religious activities

	Very Favorable	Favorable	Mixed Feelings	Unfavorable	Very Unfavorable	Never Heard of it
1) Quiet Mass with no responses	1	2	3	4	5	6
2) Mass with responses; no singing	1	2	3	4	5	6
3) Participation Mass with singing	1	2	3	4	5	6
4) Guitar Mass; Contemporary hymns	1	2	3	4	5	6
5) Informal Masses in homes	1	2	3	4	5	6
6) The "Kiss of Peace" in Mass	1	2	3	4	5	6
7) Laymen receiving Communion in the hand	1	2	3	4	5	6
8) Baptisms during Mass	1	2	3	4	5	6

)) Communal Penance services	1	2	3	4	5	6
)) Prayer Groups	1	2	3	4	5	6
)) Benediction; Evening devotions	1	2	3	4	5	6
)) Laymen distributing Holy Communion	1	2	3	4	5	6
) Other (please specify)	1	2	3	4	5	6

24. Please indicate the amount of help the Church has given you through sermons, study groups, counseling, etc. on the topics listed below. Circle the number under the heading most closely reflecting your experience.

	Very Helpful	Helpful	Of Little Help One Way or Another	Somewhat Unhelp-ful	Very Unhelp-ful	Other (please specify)
) Guidance in personal prayer life	1	2	3	4	5	6
) Guidance for family and marital relations	1	2	3	4	5	6
) Guidance for conduct on the job	1	2	3	4	5	6
) Guidance on social and political issues	1	2	3	4	5	6
) Guidance in forming my religious beliefs	1	2	3	4	5	6

25. If your parish priests took a public stand in their sermons on each of the following topics, what would your reactions be? Circle the number in each column most closely expressing your feelings.

Topic	Strongly Approve	Approve	Mixed Feelings	Dis-approve	Strongly Dis-approve	Depends on Circum-stances	No Opinion
) Business ethics	1	2	3	4	5	6	7
) Problems faced by welfare recipients	1	2	3	4	5	6	7

3)	Pollution of our environment	1	2	3	4	5	6	7
4)	School busing	1	2	3	4	5	6	7
5)	Giving to charity	1	2	3	4	5	6	7
6)	Vietnam War	1	2	3	4	5	6	7
7)	Upbringing of children	1	2	3	4	5	6	7
8)	Women's Liberation	1	2	3	4	5	6	7

26. Local churches react in different ways to social, economic, and political issues. In which of the following ways do you feel the local parish should respond to these issues? If you wish, you may check more than one

_____1) Encourage individuals to form parish discussion groups on public policy issues
_____2) Take official stands on public policy issues
_____3) Allow church facilities to be used by social action groups
_____4) Encourage individuals to form unofficial parish social action groups
_____5) Encourage individuals to participate in community social action groups
_____6) None of the above
_____7) Other (please specify)_____

27. Please check the statement which comes closest to your understanding of the Bible.

_____1) Scripture is literally true.
_____2) Scripture is not literally true but is the most important way of knowing about God.
_____3) Scripture is one of many equally important ways of knowing about God.
_____4) Scripture is less important than other ways of knowing about God.
_____5) Scripture is of very little importance.
_____6) Other (please specify) _____

28. Please check any of the following which you think are sacred. If you wish, you may check more than one.

_____1) The Ten Commandments   _____7) Christmas
_____2) The Eucharist   _____8) Easter
_____3) Freedom   _____9) Memorial Day
_____4) A church sanctuary   _____10) Sunday
_____5) Love   _____11) A human being
_____6) The Bible   _____12) Other (please specify

29. As an adult, have you ever had an experience of the presence of God?

  ____1) I'm sure I have.   ____3) I don't think so.
  ____2) I think I have.   ____4) I'm sure I have not.

30. Check those activities in the following list which you would consider to be worship. If you wish, you may check more than one.

  ____1) A religious discussion group ____ 7) Sunday service in
  ____2) A group hymn sing   church
  ____3) Personal devotions   ____ 8) Performance of
  ____4) Communion with nature   great music
  ____5) Devotions connected with a ____ 9) A prayer group meeting
     church program or activity ____10) Study and reflection
  ____6) Sharing common concerns ____11) An outdoor church service
     with a caring group   ____12) Other (Please specify)
                    _____

31. Some people say that they do not really feel comfortable in church. Do you ever feel uncomfortable for any of the following reasons? If you wish, you may check more than one.

  ____1) I have religious doubts (for example about prayer or about God).
  ____2) I do not feel comfortable with the other members; they are not the kind of people I would pick as my friends.
  ____3) I do not agree with what the priest(s) preaches or tries to do.
  ____4) Changes have taken away many of the things the Church has stood for.
  ____5) Church rituals and liturgies are outmoded.
  ____6) Church creeds and doctrines are outmoded.
  ____7) Other (please specify)_____
  ____8) I never feel uncomfortable in church.

Social Attitudes and Activities

1. Are you a member of any voluntary organizations besides church groups?

  1) Yes____   2) No____

  1a. If yes, please list the groups and indicate the approximate number of hours per month you spend in connection with the group.

                   Approximate
    Name of Group   Hours per Month

  _____   _____
  _____   _____
  _____   _____
  _____   _____
  _____   _____

2. What is your opinion of the neighborhood in which you live?

_____1) Very favorable   _____4) Unfavorable
_____2) Favorable   _____5) Very unfavorable
_____3) Mixed feelings   _____6) No opinion

3. How do you feel about America's future?

_____1) Very optimistic   _____5) Very pessimistic
_____2) Somewhat optimistic   _____6) I am confused and
_____3) Mixed feelings   uncertain
_____4) Somewhat pessimistic   _____7) No opinion

4. What is your political preference?

_____1) Democratic   _____5) Republican
_____2) Independent, leaning toward   _____6) Independent, leaning
Democratic   toward Republican
_____3) Strictly independent   _____7) No political preference
_____4) American Independent Party   _____8) Other (please specify)
(Wallace)   _____

5. In general, which of the following ways of making family decisions do you think is most desirable?

_____1) The husband should make the major decisions.
_____2) The wife should make the major decisions.
_____3) The husband and wife together should make the major decisions.
_____4) The parents should jointly make the major decisions, but only after consulting the children.
_____5) The whole family, parents and children, should make the major decisions.
_____6) Other (please specify) _____

6. In terms of morality, do you believe that life today is getting better or worse?

_____1) Better
_____2) Worse
_____3) About the same
_____4) Don't know

7. Which of the following is the most important thing for a child to learn to prepare himself for life? (Please check only one.)

_____1) To obey
_____2) To be well-liked or popular
_____3) To think for himself
_____4) To work hard
_____5) To help others when they need help

8. How often do the following statements apply to you? Circle the
    number under the heading which best describes your experience.

	Very Often	Often	Some-times	Not Very Often	Never
I find myself so pressed for time that I do not stop and help someone when I know I should.	1	2	3	4	5
I trade help and favors back and forth with my friends and neighbors.	1	2	3	4	5
On my own I spend time helping the less fortunate members of the parish or community.	1	2	3	4	5
I borrow money from relatives or friends rather than from a bank or other financial institution.	1	2	3	4	5
I ask myself "What is the morally _right_ thing for me to do in this situation?"	1	2	3	4	5
I give money to charitable causes outside the church.	1	2	3	4	5

9. Indicate your reaction to the following statements by circling the
    number under the heading which best expresses your feelings.

	Strongly Agree	Agree	Mixed Feelings	Disagree	Strongly Disagree	Depends on Circumstances	No Opinion
It is wrong for people to have pre-marital sexual relations.	1	2	3	4	5	6	7
It is wrong for married people to have sexual relations with persons other than their husbands or wives.	1	2	3	4	5	6	7
Divorce is wrong.	1	2	3	4	5	6	7
It is wrong for a woman who wants an abortion in the first three months of pregnancy to have one.	1	2	3	4	5	6	7

5) Drinking is wrong. 1   2   3   4   5   6   7

6) Christian princi-
ples can provide
the basis for   1   2   3   4   5   6   7
participating in
protest movements.

7) Welfare reci-
pients should be   1   2   3   4   5   6   7
put to work.

8) Our present econ-
omic system is the
best form of   1   2   3   4   5   6   7
economic organiza-
tion.

9) American involve-
ment in the Viet-
nam War has been   1   2   3   4   5   6   7
immoral.

10) Divorces in which
neither party has
to give grounds   1   2   3   4   5   6   7
for divorce should
be legalized.

11) The suburbs should
be racially inte-   1   2   3   4   5   6   7
grated.

12) Communes with
more than one
husband or wife   1   2   3   4   5   6   7
are acceptable
forms of family
life.

13) The sale of
marijuana should   1   2   3   4   5   6   7
be legalized.

14) Our present
political system
is the best form   1   2   3   4   5   6   7
of political
organization.

15) The government
should give money
to church-   1   2   3   4   5   6
sponsored schools.

6) Ideas of self-
sacrificing service
and love toward
others cannot be   1   2   3   4   5   6   7
practiced in
business and poli-
tics.

7) Young people these
days are too ideal-
istic and not in   1   2   3   4   5   6   7
touch with the real
world.

8) Some day men will
solve most of
their problems on   1   2   3   4   5   6   7
earth and live in
a peaceful world.

9) The government
should be neutral
toward religious   1   2   3   4   5   6   7
institutions.

0) Air and water
pollution is not
as big a problem
as newspapers and   1   2   3   4   5   6   7
TV would lead one
to believe.

III. General Information

Now we would like to ask you a few personal questions about yourself. Most
of these answers can be checked very quickly.

1. What is your age? (Check)

____1) Under 20   ____4) 30-34   ____7) 55-64
____2) 20-24   ____5) 35-44   ____8) 65 or over
____3) 25-29   ____6) 45-54

2. What is your sex? 1) Female____   2) Male____

3. What is your race?

____1) Black
____2) White
____3) Other (please specify) _____

4. Do you think of yourself as belonging to a particular nationality or ethnic group, such as German, Irish, etc.?

   1) Yes_____   2) No_____

   4a. If yes, which one?_____

5. Were you born in the United States? 1) Yes_____   2) No_____

6. What is your marital status?

   _____1) Married   _____4) Divorced
   _____2) Single   _____5) Separated
   _____3) Widowed

7. Do you have any children? 1) Yes_____   2) No_____

   7a. If yes, how many? _____

   7b. If yes, how many live at home? _____

   7c. If yes, how many now attend a Catholic grade school? _____
                                               Catholic high school? _____
                                               Catholic college? _____

8. How many of your <u>four</u> closest friends live within a mile of you? _____

9. What is the highest year of school you have completed?

   _____1) Some grammar school   _____4) High school graduate
   _____2) Eighth grade graduate   _____5) Some college
   _____3) Some high school   _____6) 4-year college graduate
                                          _____7) Post-graduate work

10. What is your present occupational status? (Check as many as apply.)

   _____1) Employed full-time   _____5) Student full-time
   _____2) Employed part-time   _____6) Homemaker full-time
   _____3) Unemployed at present   _____7) Other (please specify)
   _____4) Retired   _____

11. What kind of work does the major wage earner in your family do? (If retired, please answer on the basis of previous occupation.) Please be as specific as possible, such as plumber, electrician, insurance agent, electrical engineer, secretary, etc.

_____

12. What is your present yearly total family income before taxes?

_____1) Under $5,000   _____4) $15,000 to 19,999
_____2) $5,000 to 9,999   _____5) $20,000 to 24,999
_____3) $10,000 to 14,999   _____6) $25,000 to 49,999
                                     _____7) $50,000 and over

Please feel free to make any additional comments on this page.

_____

_____

_____

_____

_____

_____

_____

_____

        Thank you for your time and patience. Please go over the questionnaire
to make sure you have answered every question. Place the questionnaire in
the pre-addressed envelope and mail it to us. If you have any questions
about any part of the questionnaire, do not mail the questionnaire now. Wait
for a member of the Center for the Scientific Study of Religion staff to
telephone you. The staff member will explain any such questions.

                        The pastor and the CSSR

STUDIES IN RELIGION AND SOCIETY

edited by

Thomas C. Campbell, W. Alvin Pitcher,
W. Widick Schroeder and Gibson Winter

Other CSSR Publications in the Series:

Paul E. Kraemer, AWAKENING FROM THE AMERICAN DREAM, 1973

William C. Martin, CHRISTIANS IN CONFLICT, 1972

Victor Obenhaus, AND SEE THE PEOPLE, 1968

Walter M. Stuhr, Jr., THE PUBLIC STYLE: A STUDY
OF THE COMMUNITY PARTICIPATION OF PROTESTANT MINISTERS, 1972

W. Widick Schroeder, et al., SUBURBAN RELIGION: CHURCHES
AND SYNAGOGUES IN THE AMERICAN EXPERIENCE, 1974

Lawrence Witmer, ed., ISSUES IN COMMUNITY ORGANIZATION, 1972

Order from the Center for the Scientific Study of Religion

Other Books in the Series:

Thomas C. Campbell and Yoshio Fukuyama, THE FRAGMENTED LAYMAN, 1970

John Fish, BLACK POWER/WHITE CONTROL:
THE STRUGGLE OF THE WOODLAWN ORGANIZATION IN CHICAGO, 1973

John Fish, et al., THE EDGE OF THE GHETTO, 1968

W. Widick Schroeder and Victor Obenhaus,
RELIGION IN AMERICAN CULTURE, 1964

Gibson Winter, RELIGIOUS IDENTITY, 1968

Order from your bookstore

Notes about the author. . . .

Thomas P. Sweetser, S.J. is the director of the Parish
Evaluation Project, an organization that assists parishes
in learning and responding to the needs of their people.
He also teaches at the Institute for Pastoral Studies, a
department of Loyola University in Chicago. He is co-
author of SUBURBAN RELIGION: CHURCH AND SYNAGOGUES IN
THE AMERICAN EXPERIENCE and has published articles in
Chicago Studies, Cross and Crown, The New Catholic World
and People.

Fr. Sweetser was educated in both sociology and theology.
He received an M.A. in sociology from the University of
Minnesota and an M.A. in theology from Loyola University.
He received his Th.D. from Chicago Theological Seminary
in a program of study combining sociology and theology.

He is a Jesuit priest of the Wisconsin Province, currently
living in Chicago, Illinois.